BAIL OUT OVER NORTH AFRICA

America's First
Combat Parachute
Missions
1942

By

William Pelham Yarborough

Also by the same author:
Trial in Africa, Heritage Foundation, 1976
Bail Out Over North Africa, Phillips Publications, 1979,
2nd edition, 2000
International Military & Defense Encyclopedia (contributor), 1993
MacMillan Encyclopedia of the American Military (contributor), 1994
If We Really Want a Volunteer Army, Phillips Publications, 2000

Second Edition
March 2000

Library of Congress Catalogue Card 79-50900
ISBN — O-932572-06-5

Printed in the United States of America.
Phillips Publications, P.O. Box 168, Williamstown, New Jersey
08094
Phone: 609-567-0695 — Fax: 609-561-4967

II.

Washington, D.C., 1979

To whom it may concern:

The Company of military Historians through its Reviewing Board takes pride in sponsoring "Bail Out Over North Africa" as a useful reference in American Military History.

Paul Patterson
President

Reviewing Board:
Albert Hoarmann
Fitzhugh McMaster
William Reid

Official:
Fitzhugh McMaster

III.

The author, as a Captain in the 501st Parachute Battalion, Ft. Benning, Georgia, 1941.

TABLE OF CONTENTS

INTRODUCTION
To Second Edition
Bail Out Over North Africa
by
Colonel Lee Mize, U.S. Army Special Forces
Congressional Medal of Honor

The author is very clear in *Bail Out Over North Africa* of the need for a Special Operations Command.

Examples:

1. The change of plans at "H" hour and the failure of supporting units being notified of this change.

2. The British ship operating on the wrong beacon channel, leaving the AAF without navigational aid, needed in order for the Air Force C-47's to be guided to their drop zones.

3. The Air Force was not trained nor equipped for this type of special operation.

Those are only three of many examples that should have awakened the military leadership that our forces needed a Special Operations Command.

After World War II, this outstanding officer's career was placed on hold for reasons known only to the "Puzzle Palace" (Pentagon). In the late 1950's and early 1960's events, taking place in Southeast Asia (Vietnam) gave Colonel Yarborough the dream of his life. He was assigned as the Commander, Special Warfare Center, Ft. Bragg, North Carolina. B.G. Yarborough, upon taking command, saw the need for change in Special Forces Groups, Special Warfare Training Group, Psychological Warfare units and Civil Affairs units.

Within his command, he changed all units' primary missions of unconventional warfare (UW), to counter-insurgency (CI) warfare. This was accomplished to meet the need of upcoming

A, B & C detachments to Southeast Asia. Special Forces Training Group had to make major changes in their mission from the role of UW to CI.

Due to the untiring leadership of this fine officer, mission changes were accomplished in a very short time. He developed the Operations and Intelligence course (O & I). He made that the most outstanding training course for senior NCO's in the entire U.S. Army. The Special Forces soldiers that were trained in his command were the best in our armed forces.

The requests for additional A & B detachments to assist the other missions in Southeast Asia was depleting Special Forces of their operational personnel. General Yarborough was given permission to organize two additional Special Forces Groups in order to meet the Army's requirements.

The SF units that he sent to Southeast Asia performed outstanding throughout that long war. Legendary individual and group achievements will be written about in military history for years to come.

Commanders in our Army today, especially those of flag status, can thank General Yarborough for his untiring effort in working for a Special Operations Command. Years of effort were made to bring Special Forces, Ranger and Air Commandos under one umbrella of command. His dream came about, but it was after his retirement from the U.S. Army.

Throughout his military career, his lovely wife, Norma, was always beside him. She gave him the support to overcome any task. Everyone who met her loved this wonderful lady.

I thank LTG and Mrs. Yarborough for letting me be a part of the Special Forces history during his tenure of command.

INTRODUCTION

How proud I am to have had an advance look at Bill Yarborough's book "Bail Out Over North Africa". This is a thrilling and authentic account by one of the finest soldiers I was associated with in World War II.

As Deputy Commander to General Eisenhower, I was in charge of the TORCH joint British and American planning in London. Bill Yarborough (now Lieutenant General Yarborough, US Army, Retired) was on my staff and principal advisor on Airborne matters. I spent many hours with Bill and Ed Raff, the Commander of the 509th Parachute Battalion, discussing possible uses of their paratroopers in our landings in North Africa. The Battalion executed what was probably the most dangerous, complicated and longest air drop in history. Yet, both Yarborough and Raff unhesitatingly supported this mission and carried it out with superb skill and courage.

I take this opportunity to pay tribute to the gallant, competent paratroopers of this organization and, in particular, their leaders. These men couldn't wait to get into battle and they did it the hard way, by literally jumping into the midst of the fray, and always accomplished their mission. It is true that their initial drop in North Africa was made more complicated because of the lack of opportunity for sufficient advanced planning between the paratroopers and the Air Force pilots whose planes carried out the mission.

The gallant men of the 509th were determined to meet their objective, and in so doing to advance another foot, to fire another shot, and to die if need be, in defense of the principles they held so dear. This was invariably true when Yarborough and Raff were out in front leading them every step of the way.

Never did a Commander have more to be proud of than I, when during the difficult and long Italian Campaign, I had included in my Fifth Army the gallant 509th Parachute Battalion, to which I assigned important and dangerous missions, all of which they accomplished, thereby contributing to the final surrender of the German Ground Forces which had confronted us for so long in the mud and mountains of Italy.

Mark W. Clark
General, US Army, Retired

The author receives the handshake of General Mark W. Clark, Commanding General, USFA who has just decorated Colonel Yarborough with the Silver Star. 10 July, 1945.

(Photo by Kleinerman, 3131 Signal Photo Platoon)

FOREWORD

William Pelham Yarborough was one of the pioneers of America's airborne effort during and after World War II. Graduating from West Point in the class of 1936, the brand new Second Lieutenant was assigned to the 57th Infantry, Philippine Scouts. In 1940, his adventurous spirit was to bring him back to the States to join the first parachute battalion to be formed in America. Although the new parachute program was already underway, it did not take Lt. Yarborough long to become a vital part of the program. He soon became a company commander, test officer for parachute equipment and intelligence officer. He also became one of the advisors and "stand-in" actors for "Parachute Battalion", the first movie made on the new airborne.

As the test officer, he added many items to the airborne. He designed both the jump boots and the parachute wings, the two most valued possessions of a paratrooper. This feat alone would be enough to forever endear him in the hearts of all troopers to follow, even though until recently they had no idea as to just who the actual hero was. There were many contributions to the early paratrooper's equipment by Captain Yarborough that would prove to be important for survival in combat, but for the average trooper, these two symbols -- the boots and wings --would forever be the most important. They were proof to all that the wearer was something mighty special, the finest soldier going.

Called to England in July 1942 as General Mark Clark's airborne planning officer, he not only made the plans for the airborne aspects of the invasion of North Africa, but became highly involved with the British Airborne, resulting in the high rapport between the two countries' parachute units.

Major Yarborough was Executive Officer of the Parachute Task Force and flew along with the troops of the 509. The events laid out in this book are the most accurate account of the American Paratroop Force prior to and in North Africa to date.

As the paratroopers' part of the campaign came to its natural end, Yarborough reported back to General Clark for a new assignment. One of those assignments found him leading a battalion in the airborne invasion of Sicily.

As a Lieutenant Colonel, he once again rejoined the 509th Parachute Infantry Battalion, this time as its Commanding Officer, after the previous C.O., Lt. Col. Doyle Yardley, was wounded and captured during the Avellino drop in Italy. Yarborough asked for this command even though the men were still behind the German lines and no one in the 5th Army Headquarters knew how many men would survive, if any. Having been a part of the battalion and involved in their training, he had absolute confidence in the men and their abilities. There was never any doubt in his mind that most all would fight their way out.

Regrouping the battalion after over two thirds did indeed report back, and integrating the new replacements into the existing companies, he started preparing the battalion for the battles ahead. The outstanding achievements of the 509 surely attest to his leadership and skill in training men for combat.

Having served under him in World War II as a common G.I., I know that he never hesitated to put himself through the same risks his men had to take. He instilled into the men of his command a sense of pride in their fellow members, their unit and in themselves. We, the men, had that same pride in him, but most important, complete confidence in his leadership.

After leading the battalion through three major battles in Italy at Venafro and Anzio, and the Southern France invasion, and continuing the latter campaign on up to the Italian Alps, he left the battalion to attend a short course at the Command and General Staff College in 1944. He returned to Italy where he took command of the 473rd Infantry Regimental Combat Team which fought its way up the Ligurian Coast, captured Genoa, then advanced to the French Border as the War came to an end.

His heart remained with the 509th even though his new command had brought with it promotion to the rank of full Colonel.

He retired from the Army as a Lieutenant General, August 1, 1971.

I am extremely pleased to have had the opportunity not only to have served under Bill Yarborough, but also for this chance to say a few words about him and his book, "Bail Out Over North Africa."

Charles H. Doyle
Kingston, Mass.
July 4, 1979

Pfc. Charles H. Doyle - 509th Parachute Infantry - during WWII.

Acknowledgements

The author wishes to extend his thanks to the following individuals for their assistance with *Bail Out Over North Africa*:

General Mark W. Clark — Charleston, S.C.
Colonel Lee Mize — Gaston, Ala.
Bonnie Baker — Berlin, N.J.
Arthur Bakley — Camden, N.J.
Rodger Bell — Society for the Studies of the E.T.O. — England
Paul Benedetti — Hammonton, N.J.
Denzel Brittan — Upper Darby, Pa.
Theodore Z. Davis — Camden, N.J.
Everett Dennis, Jr. — Egg Harbor City, N.J.
Charles H. Doyle — Kingston, Mass.
Paul S. Frye — Turnersville, N.J.
John Howe — Camden, N.J.
Gene Litz — Medford, N.J.
Marie Martin — Lindenwold, N.J.
Eleanor Meany — Philadelphia, Pa.
Victor Rovani — Hammonton, N.J.
Dina White — Folsom, N.J.
Jacqueline White — Folsom, N.J.
Jeanne Rubba Witzig — Berlin, N.J.
Tammy Owings — Landrum, S.C.
Rainey Yearwood — Greenville, S.C.
Kathy Wolfe — Greer, S.C.

First Lady Eleanor Roosevelt and Lt. Col. Edson Raff inspect the paratroopers of the 2/503 at Hungerford, England, 3 November, 1942.

Note: Both jumpers wear the M-1942 jumpsuit designed by the author. Both have individually camouflaged their jump helmets. Trooper on the right has painted his jumpsuit. Trooper on the left wears unit made ammo pouches. To the right of trooper #2 is the first bayonet ever made for the M-1 Carbine. A British-made product fashioned at a local aircraft factory for Lt. Col. Raff.

Chapter I

Dark Days For The Allied Powers

In the spring of 1942, the world-wide strategic situation of the Allied Powers looked bleak. Virtually all of the Western European area was either in the hands of the Axis Forces or was dominated by them. The Germans were on the outskirts of Moscow -- halted for the moment, but not lacking in equipment, reserves or will to win.

In the Libyan Desert, the British defeat at Tobruk was added to the list which already included Dunkirk, Hong Kong and Singapore. Rommel's Afrika Corps had not yet begun to worry too much about Montgomery's British Eighth Army. After all, behind Rommel, stretching all the way across the North African Continent to the Atlantic Ocean, was Axis territory.

On the high seas and in the Mediterranean, the picture was equally somber from the Allied point of view. In March of 1942 alone, over a half million tons of Allied shipping was destroyed by enemy submarine action. This figure rose to an even more alarming level in May of the same year. British convoys entering the Mediterranean through the narrow Straits of Gibraltar escaped from the hostile submarine packs in the Atlantic only to run into Italian and German land-based aircraft flying from fields in Italy, Sicily and North Africa. Besieged Malta was supported by sea only at a great cost in lives and shipping - and to the tune of incredible gallantry on the part of the ships' crews and their escorts.

American strategic estimates aimed at producing plausible courses of action against Germany and her Axis partners invariably pointed in a single direction. The Allies would be forced to seek the ultimate military victory in Europe. As far as the Anglo-American forces were concerned, the British Isles were the only logical launching base for their major effort.

In April of 1942, the British and United States' governments officially agreed upon a cross-Channel strategy. From that time forward, it became the central theme for the entire planning process.

The shocking losses of Allied shipping together with the global nature of the war represented major considerations in the development of Allied strategy. No matter how brilliantly conceived, massive military action against the widely deployed and powerful Axis forces required shipping -- plenty of it!

Once their strategic concept was firm, the Allied planners went to work to earmark and stockpile the astronomical amounts of supplies, equipment and transportation which would be needed. Even the most optimistic estimates showed that a meaningful cross-Channel operation could not possibly take place before the end of 1943, or more probably, in early 1944. The fact was that the major portion of the essential materiel did not yet exist.

As planning progressed, it became quite clear that unless there was almost complete concentration on preparation for the European invasion, even the 1944 target could not be met. Indeed, if the Channel was to be crossed in force at all, a number of minor miracles would have to be performed.

It was while they were struggling with this sobering factual environment, that the Allied strategic planners were forced to submit to mounting psychological pressures urging them to open up a second fighting front.

Both the British and American press began to hammer monotonously on the "Second Front" theme. The Soviet Union, under heavy military attack, provided expert propaganda ammunition to the mass media. Since these materials reflected the fears and anguish of the Russian people and were in response to a real danger, they were given wide circulation in the United States and Britian.

General Eisenhower, at the center of the planning process, noted with apprehension the growing public clamor for a second front. For security reasons, it was not prudent to advise the press that the Allies did not have the means to launch a successful offensive at that time. The enemy would have been delighted to have had confirmation of such a predicament from "official" announcements.

It was primarily in response to artificially stimulated public sentiment that President Roosevelt finally ordered the Joint Chiefs of Staff to take some kind of measures which would ease the clamor.

In his book "Crusade in Europe", General Eisenhower listed three courses of action which appeared to have merit. These were:

a. To reinforce the British Armies fighting Rommel in Libya.
b. To conduct limited objective operations in northwest France for the purpose of seizing and holding a beachhead which could be used later when the cross-Channel invasion began.
c. To mount amphibious operations against northwest Africa and from bases established there, move east to trap Rommel.

Winston Churchill's support for the last course of action seems to have clinched the deal. The North African operation was approved on 24 July 1942 and given the code name "Torch".

General Eisenhower made the strongest point that Torch was a hurry-up affair in response to psychological and political pressure. He noted that it represented a violent shift in targets and timing at the expense of the cross-Channel strategy, and that it was "diversionary" in character.

The North African venture would, however, not be a waste of effort in any way other than with respect to its logistical impact upon the preparations for the attack on *Festung Europa*. The latter operation would by code-named "Overlord".

There were several positive advantages which would stem from Torch. These included:

a. The opening of the Mediterranean to Allied shipping.
b. The relief of Malta.
c. Elimination of the Cape route to the Middle East and India.

11.

d. U.S. troops would be given a chance to get some fighting and logistic experience in a secondary theater before facing the main event on the Continent of Europe.

General Mark Wayne Clark had gone to the United Kingdom in June of 1942 for the purpose of commanding the U.S. II Corps which was earmarked for the cross-Channel invasion. Once the North African operation had been decided upon, Clark became Eisenhower's deputy for the Torch operation.

Paratroopers train in England on obstacles and smoke, getting ready for the first combat mission in Africa (Z. Rosenfeld).

The author at No. 1 Cumberland Place, London, England, in October 1942, during the planning for the Parachute Task Force.

The newly developed radar beacon ''Eureka'' was tested from the roof of this building to see whether American troop carrier aircraft could pick up the homing signal.

Chapter II

American Paratroops Take on
a "Hare-Brained" Mission

Upon my return in 1940 from three years' service with a Philippine Scout Regiment stationed near Manila, I had joined the 501st Parachute Battalion at Fort Benning, Georgia. As our Paratroops were in their infancy and there had been minimal United States experience in military parachuting, our search for training guidance focused upon foreign paratroop developments, particularly those of Germany and of the Soviet Union. After commanding a Parachute Company and following a stint as a Parachute Test Officer of the Provisional Parachute Group, I became Intelligence Officer of the Airborne Command. While in the latter role, I was asked by the War Department to accept an assignment to the Soviet Union as an Assistant Military Attaché for the purpose of gathering all possible data on Russian parachute troops.

This took me to Washington, D.C. where I underwent a long series of briefings and preparations for attaché duty. I then settled down to wait for my Soviet visa to come through. It was during this waiting period which stretched into several weeks, that I received word from General Clark. His proposition was simple and direct. He wanted me to join him in England to fill the slot of Airborne Planner on his staff. I had had enough of the Russian delaying tactics and accepted Clark's invitation enthusiastically. I arrived in England in July of 1942, and went to work in Norfolk House.

The 2nd Battalion 503rd Parachute Infantry (later to have its designation changed to the 509th Parachute Battalion) had preceded me to the UK by a month.

In spite of elaborate security precautions aimed at protecting the identity and strategic potential of the Battalion, its arrival in England had been duly announced over Radio Berlin by the British renegade "Lord Haw Haw". Not only was an *ersatz* welcome extended to the American paratroop unit as a whole, but Lord Haw Haw also announced accurately the name of its commander, Lieutenant Colonel Edson Duncan Raff, together with names of a number of other ranks. The effect on the Yanks was electric. Some began to suspect Nazi agents were among them.

Not long after the Berlin broadcast, British and American journalists picked up the scent. American paratroops in Britain became fair game for news stories and pictures. This effectively put two strikes on any chance of obtaining strategic surprise in connection with paratroop operations on the Continent.

Ed Raff was a superb soldier. I had known him first at West Point where we had been on the swimming team together. I had also seen a lot of him at Fort Benning in the early Airborne days when new parachute battalions were being formed in rapid succession. He was a tough disciplinarian, fearless, aggressive and tenacious. He always kept himself in top physical condition and in the stamina department was more than a match for any man in his unit. Those of us who knew him well had complete confidence in his soldierly qualities. He was to prove his worth repeatedly under some of the most difficult combat situations.

Raff's battalion was quartered on the estate of American-born Lady Ward at Chilton Foliat, near Hungerford in Berkshire. The American paratroopers plunged directly and vigorously into an intensive training program. In the process, the Yanks adopted some of the British techniques and items of equipment. As the weeks passed, the Battalion began to acquire an enviable reputation.

Its members ran through the difficult British obstacle courses faster than they had ever been negotiated before. From the Tommies, the Americans learned the secret of rapid and sustained stiff-legged marching. They fired high explosives from their mortars and threw live hand grenades, many of them for the first time. Little by little they were making up for the realism which had been lacking in their training in the United States.

While the 2nd Battalion 503rd Parachute Infantry was getting itself ready for whatever mission it would ultimately be assigned,

I was busy learning to be a high level staff planner. This involved liaison with both our own and Allied staffs.

During the process of making contact with British Forces and getting read-in on the overall environment in the United Kingdom, I went through the British Parachute School at Ringway just outside Manchester. There I made several jumps from captive balloons and from the circular jump hatches of British Whitley Bombers. I was also able to lay the groundwork for gaining access to that part of the British Intelligence System which supported their parachute operations. This contact was invaluable when our own operational planning began to gather momentum.

It was early September of 1942 when General Clark called me to his office in Norfolk House and told me of the overall concept for "Torch". I had, up until this point, been working on the Airborne aspects of an operation called "Sledgehammer" which had as its objective parachute landings on the Normandy Peninsula to seize a beachhead.

General Clark pulled the curtains open behind his desk, revealing a wall map of North Africa. Large arrows showed attack directions for three task forces. He explained the significance of each to me.

There was first the "Western Task Force" which would sail directly from the United States and would take the port of Casablanca. It would then occupy French Morocco. Farther to the east, inside the Mediterranean, another arrow represented the "Center Task Force" which would take Oran. Still farther to the east was the "Eastern Task Force", a predominantly British effort which would capture Algiers and then drive for Tunis.

It was the "Center Task Force" aimed at Oran that Clark wanted to talk about particularly. Within the tactical area of the CTF were two French airfields of considerable importance. They were the only good airfields in all of Western Algeria. Their names, Tafaraoui and La Senia were to become as familiar

17.

to me as my own before the campaign was over.

Tafaroui was the only hard surfaced airfield from the Atlantic Coast of Morocco to Algiers. It was obvious that enemy aircraft flying from Tafaroui and La Senia could constitute an almost fatal threat to the success of Torch, particularly in the Oran-Algiers area. It was equally apparent that the Allied air units would need the two airfields when our troops were ashore. The first aircraft to arrive would be our fighters flying from their overcrowded staging stop at Gibralter.

La Senia was about five miles south of Oran, and Tafaroui was some ten miles farther south. Both fields were too distant from the invasion beaches to make them feasible early objectives for the amphibious forces.

Bombing La Senia and Tafaroui in order to interrupt their use by hostile forces would serve to convince the French garrisons that we did not come as allies but as enemies. Destruction of the ground facilities would make our own air operations from the two fields more difficult. To General Clark, the use of paratroops to seize, immobilize and hold La Senia and Tafaroui, seemed a logical and legitimate application of the skills and potential of airborne forces. It was my advice as his Airborne Planner, that he now sought.

The notes I made in a first evaluation of the overall proposition looked something like this:

DEBITS

1. No paratroop operations have ever been attempted over a distance of more than four hundred miles - the most usual distance being about two hundred and fifty miles. Would the paratroops be fit to fight after a nine or ten hour flight without oxygen at 10,000 feet?

2. The aircraft which we are to use, are not fitted with blackout curtains, flame dampeners for the exhausts, nor with night navigation lights invisible from the ground.

3. There are few, if any, celestial navigators available for use

with our transports. Could our pilots hit what was essentially a point target, flying at night over fifteen hundred miles of unmarked and hostile land and sea areas?

4. The unarmed transports will have to fly without fighter protection due to the distance involved.

CREDITS

1. Since the distance from Land's End to Oran is so great, surprise may be obtained through a possible enemy failure to consider such an operation feasible.

2. The landing of five hundred fully equipped and trained men behind the enemy lines at the strategic center of his defense, may exert a tremendous effect on his morale.

3. The transport airplanes are going to be needed urgently in connection with further operations in Africa, and they might as well be flown there loaded with paratroopers as with freight.

4. With three months in which to train navigators and with mechanical navigational aids, finding the drop zones should not be impossible.

5. If the flight is made at night, fighter protection will not be necessary.

I was ready to give the General my answer, and I did so.

The Parachute Battalion Commander, Ed Raff, was enthusiastic about the task when I relayed General Clark's decision to him. General Clark later said that one of the few encouraging things about the entire preparation for the African venture was the unshakeable belief on the part of the paratroops, that they could and would complete their mission.

In contrast to the paratroops' eagerness to tackle the strategic venture was the pessimism of two Air Corps members of the American Planning Staff at Norfolk House. Colonel Hoyt S. Vandenberg, who was later to become Chief of Staff of the U.S. Air Force, declared that the long range airborne exercise had little chance of success. He held further that the transport aircraft were needed for logistical support of air operations and that the probability of losses connected with aerial delivery of combat troops meant that the contemplated mission should be disapproved. Echoing and supporting Colonel Vandenberg's view was Lieutenant Colonel Lauris Norstadt, who would, in time, become Supreme Allied Commander of NATO. But there was also a powerful supporter, also an Air Corps officer, whose fame stemmed from his daring raid over Japan during the darkest days of America's involvement in World War II. Major General James Doolittle thought the idea of a long-range paratroop assault against strategic targets in North Africa was a great one. It was probably Jimmy Doolittle's whole-hearted support that had helped more than any to make up General Clark's mind to go ahead with the exercise when even General Eisenhower probably considered it to be somewhat "hare-brained". But if it was indeed "hare-brained", some precedents had already been set in other theaters by American strategic planners. One of these had been the dispatch of 14,000 American troops aboard the Queen Mary to the southwest Pacific without escort in 1941. Moreover, the Queen Mary on her solitary and dangerous voyage had even stopped enroute for fuel at Rio de Janeiro where Axis spies abounded.

By comparison, our planned parachute assault into North Africa seemed to be measurably less risky.

C-47 aircraft of the 60th Troop Carrier on parachute maneuvers somewhere in England.

U.S. Army Photograph

Chapter III

Plans, Training and
Problems for the
Paratroop Task Force

The 509th Parachute Infantry Battalion is visited by a distinguished group at Chilton Foliant. Sir Winston Churchill (left) looks on as Lt. Colonel Edson D. Raff explains the display of paratrooper equipment to Mrs. Eleanor Roosevelt.

The Commanding General of the British 1st Airborne Division, Major General "Boy" Browning, stands to the right of Mrs. Roosevelt.

Training jump into an English farmer's wheat field. Note the unusually severe occilation which the decending trooper at the center of the picture must dampen in order to avoid injury upon landing.

(Photo courtesy Dr. Carlos C. Alden)

23.

The days which followed General Clark's decision were jammed with preparations of the most secret nature. A provisional Paratroop Task Force was organized under the command of Colonel William C. Bentley, U.S. Air Corps. Bentley had been the U.S. Military Attaché assigned to Tangier until a few months before his arrival in London in early 1942. Both the paratroops and the Air Corps' 60th Troop Carrier Group were placed temporarily under the Paratroop Task Force. Representatives from each unit were assigned to the Force Staff to work out the details.

The Royal Air Force provided photographs of the area in which the force would operate. British Intelligence supplied voluminous data on every imaginable item of information.

As the invasion plan took shape, it became firm that the paratroops would invade Africa as part of the Center Task Force or "CTF" under Major General Lloyd R. Fredendall. Their specific job was to capture Tafaraoui Airdrome with the Parachute Battalion, less one company, and to send that company north through Valmy to La Senia Airdrome, there to immobilize Vichy French combat aircraft. The aircraft destroyed, or otherwise immobilized, the Parachute "Saboteur" Company was then to withdraw to Tafaraoui, where it would join the remainder of the Battalion in an active defense of the Airdrome until the arrival of sea-landed Combat Command "B" of the American 1st Armored Division.

Many paratroopers knew by experience that finding a drop zone on the first pass, even in daylight, was often a very difficult task. How then, were we to find the proper spot at night with no moonlight, in strange and hostile territory? Our signal section thought it had two answers called "Rebecca" and "Eureka". These radar devices, both highly secret, had just been completed in a British electronics laboratory, and had yet to be tested under field conditions. By means of the two electronic aids, a pilot supposedly could guide his airplane to a map coordinate location even though he could not see the ground. There was one slight catch, however, The technique for using Rebecca and Eureka required someone to place Eureka physically on the spot which the pilot wished to find.

This difficult and dangerous job fell to a certain young Second Lieutenant Hapgood, Signal Corps, US Army. Hapgood was given the code name "Bantam". He looked like a scientist. He was tall and thin and walked with a slight stoop. His face was sallow from long, sunless stretches in the laboratory, and his gold-rimmed spectacles told of countless hours of delving into the theory of electronics. Hapgood habitually wore civilian clothes of indifferent tailoring. His sleeves always seemed to be at least two inches too short. The young American signaller had been sent to school in England, to learn the secrets of Rebecca and Eureka. He guarded the two brown suitcases containing the precious gadgets like the crown jewels.

The problem of getting Hapgood and his wonderful machines into North Africa was no small one in itself. Its solution involved first a discharge from the Army, and an airplane ticket back to America to throw enemy agents off the scent. Back in the United States, Hapgood would be taken in tow by our Intelligence Service, which would arrange for his clandestine entry into Algeria. We bade him goodbye one afternoon about three weeks before "D" Day. Our last glimpse of him until we met again in Algiers was of his tall, stooped figure, bent a little more under the weight of his two suitcases, struggling along Regent Street until he was finally picked up by a taxicab. Before he left the office, he had proudly showed us the little devices on each suitcase which, if activated, would blow Eureka to bits. Even the Gestapo could not put the machines together again once the destruct mechanisms had done their jobs.

In addition to Rebecca and Eureka, the Royal Navy indicated that it was also prepared to furnish us a navigational aid. This was to be in the form of a radio signal transmitted from a British merchant ship. The "Alynbank" was to sail around an elliptical course two miles long and one mile wide in the Western Mediterranean. We were given the polar coordinates of this ellipse, with respect to our drop zone. It was thought that we could pick up the ship's signal about two hundred miles off the African Coast and ride it in. Having passed the radio ship, we believed that we could fly on an azimuth which would soon bring us under Eureka's influence. The rest seemed simple. Hapgood's Algerian "underground" helpers would light ground flares when Eureka gave the signal, and we would bail out over the flares.

Over in Berkshire, Colonel Raff's war.room was established in the hall just outside his sleeping quarters. An armed guard allowed no one without a signed pass to enter. Inside, under strong overhead lights were two airdrome scale models, startlingly realistic and complete to the most minute details. On the walls were photographs of the objectives and drop zones taken from every conceivable angle and under innumerable conditions of lighting. Nowhere was the name of a town or city visible, nor was it really possible to identify the terrain with that of North Africa. Secrecy prevailed even while instruction of unit leaders was underway. Initially, the two target airdromes were called "A" and "B". Towns and roads were given similar noncommital code names.

Little groups of paratroops were constantly in the war room --sometimes a company commander and his staff, sometimes a squad leader and his squad. The tactics of the operation were discussed over and over again until every private knew what was going to happen. Each man in the Battalion was supplied with a tiny pennant bearing his name. This he was required to stick into the model at the point or points where he would find his assigned objectives. Each building, each hangar, each airplane blast shelter was discussed not once but many times. The men studying the models were able to point without hesitation to "The Operations Office at 'A' " or "The Fighter Hangars at 'B' ". Each paratroop "saboteur" knew exactly where he would slash the tail surfaces or where he was to place his incendiary grenades, in order to immobilize the Vichy airplanes which were his personal targets.

This detailed planning ran concurrently with rigid physical training which included long road marches under full combat equipment, and conditioning flights at 10,000 feet to accustom the men to protracted periods at the altitude without extra oxygen.

As time slipped by, a sudden and unforeseen complication arose. This was in the form of an order from the High Command stating that the "enemy" was not to be fired upon unless he fired first! It was even anticipated that we might land without opposition. Our diplomats in North Africa had been laboring for months to make such a peaceful occupation possible. It was further hoped that the extensive preparation which had gone into the organization of a tremendous anti-Axis underground would bear fruit. This "Fifth Column" was to arrest all known Axis sympathizers on the eve of our arrival. The friendly subversives were to take control of all utilities, to prevent sabotage at the docks, and to furnish guides for American Task Forces, once they were ashore.

To the Paratroop Force, this modification of the original plan was of considerable importance. If it was decided that we did not have to fight, we planned to air-land directly upon La Senia Airdrome, and take charge. This could be done in daylight. As convincing as the diplomats and statesmen were, the paratroops nevertheless decided to carry as much ammunition and as many grenades as they had originally intended. They were fighting men. If the enemy wished to surrender, that was up to him.

The idea that we might land unopposed was further strengthened after General Clark's historic submarine voyage to North Africa where he kept his appointment with General Charles Emmanuel Mast, then French Commander in Algiers.*

*Mark W. Clark, *Calculated Risk*, Harper & Brothers, New York, 1954.

Paratroopers of the 2nd Bn., 509th Parachute Infantry in Northern Ireland. The men are unloading parachutes and equipment from the trucks, prior to a training exercise.

(Photo courtesy Rodger Bell - Society for the Studies of the E.T.O.)

Parachutists jump during a training exercise.

28.

Inspecting the main parachute and static line during maneuvers in England 1942.

The photograph provides an excellent view of the T-5 main parachute and the reserve chest pack.

Two variations of the "jump boots" are shown in this photograph.

U.S. Army Photograph

29.

From the Paratroop Task Force level, planning progressed to the point where the take-off fields were identified. These were close to the southwest tip of England. Twenty aircraft were to depart from St. Eval and nineteen from Predannack which was only some 30 miles from Land's End.

The start of the operation was set for midnight, 8 November, 1942. After weighing the various risks which would be involved in flying over neutral Spain as compared with a course over Vichy France or the long way over the Atlantic, it was decided to go the Spanish route. We accepted the possibility that this violation of Spain's neutrality could, in the worst possible case, even bring Spain into the war on the Axis side. This risk seemed preferable to the more likely dangers of the other routes. The flight course, as we calculated it, would take eight hours if the aircraft cruised at their normal speed of 135 miles per hour. Thus if we took off at 1700 hours from Predannack and St. Eval we would be under cover of darkness from one half hour after take-off until the scheduled jump on target at 0100 hours GMT.

During the half hour of our daylight flight, our plan called for a fighter-bomber sweep of Brest and Bordeaux which we hoped would take the enemy's attention and search radar away from our slow-moving formation.

It was envisioned that our troop carriers would be escorted by Spitfires and Beaufighters as far as possible but that none would accompany us when we entered Spanish skies.

As planning and preparations went forward at an increasing pace, training was also intensified. On 26 September 1942, the 60th Transport Group flew the 2nd Battalion 503rd Parachute Infantry to Northern Ireland where they air dropped in a combined maneuver with British Forces.

Unfortunately, the Irish drop marked the end of active joint training with the troop carriers as the aircraft now began to move to the depots for modifications which were necessary for the actual mission. In addition to UHF radios, exhaust flashhiders, blackout curtains and controls for running lights, two 50 gallon gasoline drums to extend the aircrafts' fuel supply were installed just aft of the bulkhead separating the passenger from the crew compartment.

At first it had seemed that a month would be ample for the modifications to take place. This was not to be the case, however, as no priority was given by the Air Corps to the mechanical work and vital aircrew training was interrupted in a way which was almost fatal to the overall mission. Some of the troop carriers were so late leaving the depot at Burtonwood that they had only a single day to get to the take-off airfields and to prepare for the coming mission.

Even though it had been apparent from the very first that celestial navigation over Spain would be essential to the success of the Troop Carriers' part of the operation, only four sets of navigational instruments were on hand the night before take-off. It was sought to remedy this deficiency at the last minute by providing the navigators with British instruments. Unfortunately, the Americans were not familiar with this equipment. Moreover, it could not be used in the astrodomes of the C-47s.

The substantial problems reflected in lack of training and mechanical deficiencies were, for the aircrews, made even more critical because of inadequate briefings. As contrasted with the paratroop briefings which were complete to an almost microscopic degree, the aircrews received only an impromptu run-down at Aldermaston on 5 November - three days before take-off time! Even then, maps and charts were provided only to the flight leaders.

The paratroops were as ready as troops could be but their gallant young Air Corps colleagues were not ready for a variety of reasons.

Paratroops of the 2nd Bn., 509th Parachute Infantry board a C-47 for a training jump in England.

U.S. Army Photographs

U.S. paratroopers of the 2nd Bn., 509th Parachute Infantry, in a C-47 airplane which has been rigged for the flight to North Africa.

Note: Two 50 gallon gasoline drums installed just aft of the forward bulkhead. These were needed to extend the range of the C-47's.

American paratroopers of the 2d Bn. 509th Parachute Infantry emplaning for Land's End, England, where they will take off for the invasion of North Africa on the night of 7 November 1942.

U.S. Army Photograph

33.

Chapter IV

Night Flight to SNAFU

Paratroopers who will jump in North Africa, screw up their courage to face the jab of an Army medic's inoculation needle.

A final training exercise in Berkshire before movement of the 509th Parachute Infantry to Lands end.

(Photos courtesy of Dr. Carlos C. Alden)

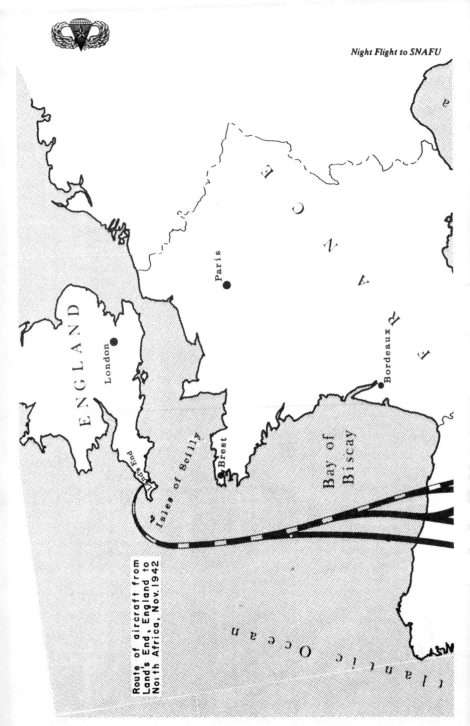

Night Flight to SNAFU

Route of aircraft from
Land's End, England to
North Africa, Nov. 1942

36.

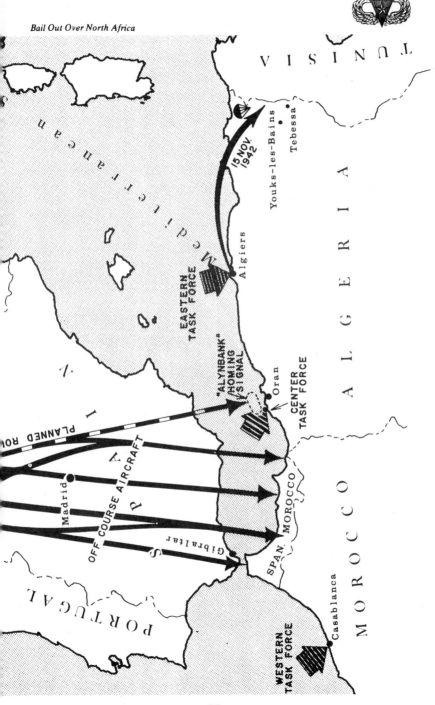

37.

Flying from Berkshire, I landed at St. Eval, the take-off air-drome near Land's End, after dark and in typical English wintry weather. Rain was driving in from the sea. I could hear the steady pounding of the surf along the wind-swept beaches in the distance.

A jeep was waiting to take me to a billet about two miles away. It was a somber three-hundred-year-old abbey overgrown with ivy.

Inside, all was warm and cheerful. Fires were burning in two huge fireplaces. The main hall was filled with paratroop officers and cigarette smoke. A radio was going full blast with music from the BBC which was audible now and then above the cacaphony of voices. Some of the officers were writing last letters home. Other more pragmatic types were checking, for the thousandth time, the mechanisms of their pistols and carbines. The group looked young, fit and enthusiastic. Morale was soaring visibly.

Getting ready for the upcoming mission was like dressing for a football game. We peeled off our service uniforms and, folding them carefully, packed them into footlockers to be sent to Quartermaster storage. We got into our parachute combat uniforms and taped the legs so that heavily laden cargo pockets would not swing back and forth as we walked. The finishing touch was a small American flag which we sewed to the left shoulder of our jump coats. We were as nearly ready for combat as we would ever be, and we were anxious to get cracking.

Every serious student of military history knows that a complicated tactical plan has more working against it than for it. Last minute changes of plan, especially where large numbers of people are involved, can throw even the most highly trained troops into confusion. It seems that the military professionals have almost as much propensity for violating these two principles as do the amateurs. Such an unfortunate event occurred at the Paratroop Task Forces "H" hour.

The battalion was scheduled to take to the air at 1730 hours if the "war plan" was in effect. If, on the other hand, it was to be the "peace plan", we would take off four hours later.

Colonel Bill Bentley, the Air Corps Commander of our Task Force, waited tensely at the radio tower for the word from the powerful British station at Gibraltar which was to set our expedition into motion.

If the code words "Advance Napoleon" came hurtling through the ether, it was to be war. If the words "Advance Alexis" were received, we would take off under the "peace" plan with the assurance that the French would not oppose our landing.

At 1700 hours, we were standing by at our airplanes in the gathering dusk. At 1710, from Gibraltar came the words "Advance Alexis". The "peace" plan was in effect!

Their adrenalin pumping, the thoroughly keyed up paratroopers and the young aircrews now had to delay departure for four hours - long enough to permit our formations to arrive over North Africa in daylight rather than under cover of darkness. Accordingly, the first aircraft took off at 2105 and by 2145 all were in the air in formation and on the way to the battle area. As our wheels raced along the runways for takeoff, I thought of the mighty ocean armada filled with Allied troops which for weeks had been approaching Africa closer and closer, and was now almost within striking distance.

Lt. Col. Ed Raff, the Paratroop Battalion Commander, rode in the second plane of the first flight in an airplane piloted by Major John Oberdorf. I flew with the 60th Group Commander, Lt. Col. Tom Schofield, in the lead airplane of Flight "B" which took off from St. Eval.

Our paratroop formation assembled in the air over Portreath then flew westward over the Scilly Islands where it turned southward toward the Bay of Biscay. Later the course was shifted to one which would take us over neutral Spain and hopefully to the vicinity of the British ship "Alynbank." It would be the Alynbank's homing signal simulating that of an Italian beacon which we hoped would then permit us to find the radar beacon "Eureka". Lieutenant Hapgood would be manning Eureka in the vicinity of Tafaraoui.

I glanced at my wrist watch -- it was now 10:15 P.M., GMT. Just about this time, our bombers would be pounding Brest and Bordeaux in order to screen our movement until we were beyond the range of the Nazi radar. I could see the navigator using a flashlight working over his charts. Very soon the cabin became cold from the altitude. At 10,000 feet, we leveled off and headed for Oran. The blankets we had brought along felt good. Most of us began to doze and eventually we fell off to sleep as the cabin lights were turned out.

Sometime about midnight I woke up. I ate a bar of chocolate and a couple of English Army biscuits. The navigator was still poring over his charts, occasionally taking a shot at the stars through the "astrodome".

In the gloom of the cabin little was visible, but I could hear the snores of the Battalion Headquarters Group. Sergeant Alain Joseph was mumbling in his sleep. I turned over and dozed off again to the drone of the motors.

About 0200 hours I woke again and peered out the window to see a city far below, brilliantly lighted. Clouds passed beneath us and obscured the winking lights from view. Just before dawn, I felt the ship bounce as it does in rough air. I could see a sheaf of fiery streamers reaching up toward us. It came to me with a start that this was "flak". We were being fired upon by ground batteries.

The airplane droned on, unhit. I watched the stream of tracers fall farther and farther to the rear.

Standing behind Colonel Tom Schofield, the pilot and Group Commander, I saw the first faint light of dawn illuminate the sky. I knew that we should be over Africa. We had been in the air for seven hours. Tensely we peered into the gloom below. A

Early morning of November 8, 1942. Six C-47 aircraft carrying elements of the 509th Parachute Infantry Battalion fly over the Mediterranean off the coast of Algeria as they head toward Tafaroui Airdrome.

One of the C-47 planeloads which landed in Spanish Morocco. Front row, left to right, first three, flight crew, names unknown, Michaels; John Boyce both Hq. Co.; James Broadway "C" Company. Second row, left to right, Garuet Porter "C" Co.; Joe Bauer, Hq. Co.; Leigh Fox, "C" Co.; Kammer, Hq. Co.; Mike Sembrat "C" Co.; William Eckroth "C" Co.

dense ground haze seemed to stretch interminably obscuring everything from view. None of our other planes was in sight.

What I did not know until later was that during the flight over the southern part of the Bay of Biscay our formation had already begun to scatter. Not more than two planes in any element or three in any flight had been able to stay together. This was partially due to clouds and to stormy weather which tossed us about considerably. The pilots were unable to use their VHF radios to keep in touch with each other effectively, as they had little or no chance to practice with them prior to the mission itself. The use of flashlights and *aldis* lamps helped some of the struggling aircraft to keep track of each other. The navigators generally had become confused to the extent that most had fallen back on "dead reckoning".

The strong easterly wind, which had not been predicted in the preflight weather report, blew most of the aircraft off course to the west 50 miles or more from their expected landfall.

One billiant edge of the sun began to show at the junction of the sea of mist and the horizon. As the light grew, the panorama below took on a fantastic appearance. Jagged rock outcroppings, gray and barren, began to poke through the swirling cloud carpet.

Silhouetted against the dazzling whiteness below, our lone airplane filled with mildly uneasy paratroopers circled looking for a hole in the clouds. "Rebecca" was dead as a mackerel and it looked as though we were invading Africa alone!

I strained my eyes for a glimpse of any recognizable terrain feature below. I could see nothing. Suddenly, I noticed with a start that there was a small black speck moving toward us from a great distance. It was coming fast, alternately appearing then disappearing among the folds and billows of the cloud blanket beneath.

I tried to keep my voice calm. "All right, men, take the plugs out of the windows and put the muzzles of your weapons through."

"If this is an enemy fighter, wait until he's close enough before you fire - he won't think this flying banana has any armament. Maybe we can fool him."

Sergeant Jack Pogue licked his thumb thoughtfully and applied it to the front sight of his Thompson submachine gun. Then he knelt down and placed the muzzle through the rubber-ringed window hole.

Sergeant Joseph's jaw was set as he squinted along the barrel of his M-1 rifle, bracing the stock against the buffeting of the slip-stream.

The dark speck grew larger as it hurtled toward us. Slowly the outline of one of our own transports became apparent. In an instant the tension vanished from the two lines of kneeling men.

"I'll bet that son of a bitch is lost," someone cracked. Everyone laughed.

Without warning, a rift appeared in our cloud floor and Schofield, seeing the ground beneath, kicked the ship into a steep bank. The other transport on our wing followed suit.

Noses pressed against windows, we saw Africa. It was brown, rocky and barren. Not a house or even a tree was visible at first. Suddenly we shot over the rim of a valley. What I saw made me swallow hard. Almost directly beneath us was one of our airplanes on the ground.

Some sort of crowd had already gathered around the troop-carrier which appeared to be resting on a small sports field. Our pilot circled and for a moment I thought he was going to land.

I pointed to a low barracks building below, from which a stream of soldiers was pouring. Another group had already formed in two ranks in front of the barracks. The glint of the morning sun on their bayonets was ominous. Schofield pulled back on his yoke and we zoomed.

In the distance off to the left I could see the blue Mediterranean. We headed for it, throttles wide open.

The pilot pointed. I saw a long streamer of dust fan out behind a tiny object bobbing along the ground. It was another of our airplanes down and trying his best to get into the air again. Smaller ribbons of dust to the rear were raised by horsemen which seemed to be bearing down upon the struggling airplane. I was glad to see the ship finally get into the air. We now had three in our formation.

Over the coast, we turned east.

We now realized that we were over Spanish Morocco, some two hundred miles from objectives and with little gasoline remaining in the tanks. As the distinctive geographic formation around Melilla passed beneath us, our exact position became clear. We were now some one hundred and forty miles west of our objectives.

We zoomed down low over the Mediterranean searching the horizons for the other ships of our Force. Soon we spotted several, flying low like ourselves and heading in the same direction. Little by little a formation began to grow.

I strained my eyes toward the panorama which was unrolling ahead as we turned inland. I could see the vast outline of the Sebkra D'Oran, a long oval-shaped salt desert which stretched from Oran to the east for thirty miles.

Suddenly I grabbed Schofield's arm and pointed to the ground ahead. There on the extreme western edge of the Sebkra were ten or twelve of our aircraft on the ground. To the north of them, scattered among the rocks of some high ground, were forty or fifty parachutes marking the spot where some of the troopers evidently had dropped.

"What do we do," yelled Schofield above the sound of the engines, "Land here or go on into Tafaraoui?"

It was obvious that things had not gone completely according to plan. At least a third to a half of our force was there on the ground beneath us. There were about ten or more airplanes in the formation our ship was now leading....

A quick decision had to be made. "Land here," I yelled, and Schofield prepared to do so.

I made my way back to the passenger compartment and briefly explained the situation.

"Take your chutes off, get your weapons ready and let's be prepared to bail out of this crate fighting if we have to."

It was just as well that we had not decided to go on to Tafaraoui, for as our wheels touched the surface of the Sebkra, the fuel gauges registered empty.

We threw the airplane door open and jumped to the ground. I tried to imagine what had happened. Along the northern edge of the Sebkra where I had seen the chutes, I could now see a column of twenty or thirty paratroops moving slowly. There were sounds of rifle and machine gun fire coming from their vicinity, but they were so far away that I couldn't tell what the circumstances were.

C-47s were all around us on the ground. Paratroops were crouched or lying under the wings of some of them. The whole picture was confused.

I walked over to a ship near ours and called to the pilot who was sitting in the exit doorway.

"What's the score," I called. "What the hell gives?"

"Damned if I know," he replied. "We were flying toward Tafaraoui when some ack-ack opened up on us. Things began to happen fast. The first thing I knew, the ship ahead of us slowed down and its load bailed out. Four or five other ships did the same thing. We came in here and landed. Our load is up there in the rocks chasing snipers."

The "Advance Alexis" code word we had received from Gibraltar the night before was supposed to have meant that we could fly right into La Senia Airdrome and land without a fight. Fighting was already in evidence around us. Therefore, the only deduction I could make was that the "War Plan" must be in effect. Something was badly snafued -- that was obvious.

I left the young aviator and continued along the edge of the Sebkra looking for Raff.

Elsewhere, the drama surrounding the Airborne phase of Torch had unfolded in a way that would take months to unravel and to interpret. Lack of adequate briefing on the Moroccan terrain together with a strong morning ground fog had added to the befuddlement of the pilots and navigators.

Three of our aircraft off course and lost had landed in Spanish Morocco. One young pilot also landed in Spanish Morocco, unloaded his paratroop passengers to save gasoline and then flew to Oran.

Two airplanes missed the landfall over the Algerian Coast due to ground fog and landed in French Morocco. One C-47 landed at Gibraltar with completely empty gas tanks.

What had happened to our navigational aids? The change from War Plan "A" to Peace Plan "B" which had delayed our takeoff from England had been partially to blame. Lieutenant Hapgood (Bantam) who had clandestinely smuggled his directional Eureka radio to the vicinity of Tafaraoui Airdrome, operated it during the time when the pre-dawn landings were expected, but when the troop carriers did not appear, he wisely destroyed the set and slunk away in the darkness dressed in an Arab burnoose. Less explainable was the failure of the British ship Alynbank to send the signal agreed upon. Directed to broadcast its beacon at 400 Kilocycles, it had unaccountably been transmitting at 460 Kilocycles and its signal was not received.

The young aircrews with their paratrooper passengers had performed a remarkable feat in just arriving in North Africa. Several, flying serenely toward what they thought were going to be peaceful landings, were attacked by anti-aircraft fire from the ground and by French fighters.

One airplane piloted by Major Clarence J. Galligan, flew through ground fire which greeted him at the Algerian Coast.

Shortly afterward, his airplane was attacked and damaged by French fighters which were driven off by Allied Spitfires and he landed on the Sebkra of Oran with his load of parachutists. The troopers promptly began to prepare a defensive position. In due course, a French Infantry Company with a seventy-five millimeter cannon accosted the little group of 14 Americans but, before there was bloodshed, Colonel Bentley, who had been the Paratroop Task Force Commander, arrived on the scene as a prisoner-of-war of the French and persuaded the small band of Americans to surrender.

Bentley had, even before the take-off from England, insisted that he could talk the French Military Garrison of Oran into "being reasonable". As Bentley had just the previous year been on the social circuit with many of the French commanders, he felt that they would listen to him. After dropping Colonel Raff over the Sebkra of Oran, Bentley had therefore chosen to disregard my advice and that of Major Oberdorf, my Air Corps assistant planner. He had flown his empty airplane to the Nor-theastern edge of the Sebkra where he landed and was picked up by the French as a prisoner only to be released upon American occupation of Oran.

Turning back the clock to 0810, Colonel Bentley with Colonel Raff aboard had engaged in another drama. This is a direct quote from the United States Air Force's account of the North African mission:

"About 0810, Bentley sighted eight planes huddled on the Sebkra near Lourmel and learned by radio of what had befallen them. At the same time, a column of armored cars was seen ap-proaching up the road from Lourmel. If they were French, the men on the Sebkra were in grave danger. Raff was eager to make a jump to meet the threat and to clear out the snipers. He held a brief radio conference with Colonel Bentley and they decided to drop the paratroops on a hill which dominated the northern edge of the Sebkra and had some cover to shield the men from enemy fire. The formation circled and nine or ten of the planes that were with Bentley dropped their sticks of paratroops."

Chapter V

Disaster in The Desert

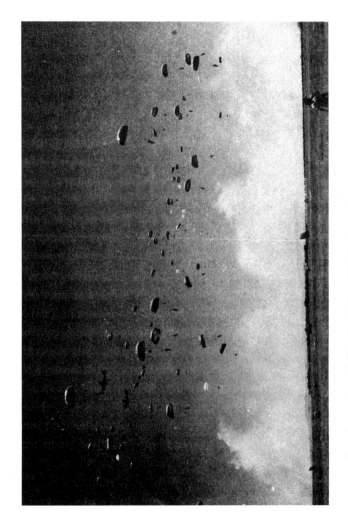

Paratroopers of the 2nd Bn., 509th Parachute Infantry landing in Algeria, 1942.

As I continued my search for Ed Raff, I could see one little group of parachutists busy removing "long handled" underwear which we had all worn under our cotton jump suits. The sun was beginning to bear down on the glaring surface of the dry salt lake.

I found Raff lying behind a pile of boulders. A medical aid man was putting strips of adhesive tape on his left side.

"What happened, Ed?" I asked.

The Colonel's face was gray with pain. There was blood at one corner of his mouth.

"I think I've busted a rib." He let out a loud groan as the aid man pressed another piece of tape into place.

"How did it happen?" I asked.

"We jumped on the high ground up there after one of our planes was fired on. Bentley saw some tanks on the ground and said they were enemy. We were almost out of gas, so we jumped. I busted a rib. The tanks belong to our combat command "B". There's one going down the road now."

The Colonel stood up and painfully put on his parachutist's jacket.

I shouted at the tank commander who had his head poked through the open turret. The vehicle swung around and stopped, its guns pointed directly at me.

"What do you guys want?" he called.

I trotted up to the tank. "We're busy as hell," the tank officer told me.

"These hills are lousy with snipers. We just knocked the crap out of a French armored car on the Oran Road. Have you seen any enemy cars down here?"

I told him that I had just landed and hadn't seen a damn thing; furthermore, that I hoped I didn't see any enemy until we got the outfit under some kind of control.

"Well, you better get it to hell off that salt bed before the Vichy fighters catch you," he said cheerfully.

"The road on the other side runs right into Tafaraoui."

"Yes, I know,"

"Some of Johnny Waters' tanks are there now. They're working on a bunch of machine gun nests over there."

"How about taking the Colonel across Sebkra?" I asked. "He's hurt and I don't think he should try to walk it."

"Can't do it, Major. I'm overdue now. I've got a date with some Frogs down thataway." He pointed toward Lourmel.

"One of our jeeps is coming along in a few minutes," he called as his tank turned down the road. "Maybe he'll take the Colonel across."

In about an hour, the battalion was moving slowly across the Sebkra. Each step was a task in itself. Just under the dry upper crust of the lake's surface was a type of plastic mud that would have immobilized a dinosaur. Our feet picked the stuff up until each shoe felt like it weighed fifteen pounds. Raff, looking green around the gills, inched past us in the jeep.

Distances in North Africa are deceptive to the eye. The Sebkra was at least eight miles wide. We were tired when we reached the south shore.

One of our communications sergeants showed me a message he had picked up. It came from a friendly airman who had just landed at Tafaraoui. He asked us to send paratroops as soon as we could. He said that there were a few enemy machine guns still firing, and that our tanks had rounded up a lot of prisoners which someone was going to have to guard.

I showed the message to Raff.

"How about it, Ed, if you give me the OK, I can slip a company in there."

"The planes are out of gas."

"Not all of them. Ours may have half an hour left even though she reads empty. If I could get three ships, we could haul about eighty men."

"OK, go ahead." He spat a blob of blood. "Let me know by

radio when you get there."

Lieutenant Joe Beck led the three transports over and set them down near us. We had taken quite a long time to get across the Sebkra, and it was getting late in the afternoon. Everybody wanted to go on the mission. Raff picked Captain Berry's Company and some of the Battalion Headquarters men.

The ships were jam-packed. We were going to fly too low to use parachutes, so the number of people in the plane didn't matter so much. Considerable weight leeway was allowed by the lack of gasoline.

We took off heavily and soon were hurtling along toward Tafaraoui at a hundred feet of altitude. I was standing just in back of Lieutenant Joe Beck, the pilot, in order to point out the spot on the airdrome on which I wished to land.

Suddenly a movement in the air to the right front caught the corner of my eye.

"What kind of planes are those, Joe?"

Joe didn't answer; he became a whirlwind. He slid into a steep bank and cut the motors. The copilot pumped the flaps down, throwing shudders through the whole ship.

My heart jumped into my throat and stayed there.

I could feel the impact as the Vichy machine gun bullets hit our ship broadside. The fuselage began to leak light as the rounds poured into the defenseless mass of men seated on the floor.

The noise was deafening. Each shot cracked so loud that I had the sensation of feeling it as well as of hearing it. I made my body as thin as I could by pressing my back against the bulkhead. I would remember to be afraid later.

We smashed into the ground going one hundred and thirty miles per hour and slewed around to a violent halt.

Again and again the murderous fire jabbed through the fuselage.

As the ship stopped, I made a rush for the open door, stepping on prostrate bodies as I did so.

I made a desperate dive onto the ground and crawled away from the damaged airplane toward a small knoll. The enemy planes were still in the vicinity and I could see the gleam of the late afternoon sun on their canopies as they banked for another run at us. As paratroops, we knew that we could expect no mercy. We got none.

The noise of the machine gun fire was coupled with the shrill sounds of the airplane motors as the attackers swooped over us again.

I buried my face in the sand. The bullets were pattering like deadly hail around us.

I lay face downward on the ground for a full minute after the last airplane had screamed over. Cautiously, I raised my head and looked around me. The three transport airplanes looked like ghosts. A paratrooper was hanging head down from the open door of our ship. Blood was slowly dripping from the ends of his fingers onto the sand.

A trooper staggered toward me with his hands stretched out like a blind man's. His face was so covered with blood I could not recognize him. I called to him to lie down and I began to shout for the aid man. The wounded man lay down near me. After I had called for the aid man two or three times, the wounded soldier told me that **he** was the aid man. Then I noticed his brassard and his medical pouch. I took a tourniquet from his pouch and put it on his arm at the elbow. I twisted the tourniquet as tightly as I could, but the blood continued to spurt from a jagged wound in his wrist. I sprinkled some sulfanilamide powder into the wound, and placed a wad of cotton on top of it.

The tourniquet needed something under it to exert more pressure on the arteries in the hollow of the trooper's elbow. I searched around in his pouch for such an object. Not finding one, I picked up a smooth stone from the desert floor and placed it under the tourniquet.

Captain (Doc) Moir was holding his hand against the side of his head. The blood was oozing from between his fingers and trickling down his elbow.

"How do you feel, Doc?" I knew it was a foolish question.

"I think I'm hit pretty badly," the parachute doctor replied calmly. "I have two in the head and one through the shoulder. The one in my shoulder stings like hell."

Sergeant Joseph was sitting dejectedly on the sand. His shin had been grazed by a machine gun bullet.

"They got Lieutenant Kunkle," he grated through clenched teeth. He pointed toward the ship.

"Look at Lieutenant Beck. He was up on top of that wing trying to check his antenna even before that last strafing run hit us."

Doc Moir was already beginning to work on the wounded in spite of the two wounds in his head and the crease in his shoulder. A paratrooper was holding another's hands above his head while a third ripped open the right side of his shirt. I could see the red gashes where the bullets had struck him.

The sun was beginning to set. Captain Berry was sobbing with rage. Lieutenant Crosby crawled painfully from the door of one of the other transports. Some of the lightly wounded men were making the others more comfortable with opened parachutes to ward off the last rays of the sun.

French Dewoitine D 520 Fighter. This was the type of fighter used by the French Air Force to attack C-47's near Tafaraoui.

Designed to meet specification issued 1937.

First prototype flew October 2, 1938.

On May 10, 1940 only Groupe de Chasse I/3 was operational with the D 520, but GC II/3, GC III/3, GC III/6, GC II/7 and naval unit 1® Flotille de Chasse became operational and joined combat before the armistice.

Between June 19th and 20th GCI/3, II/3, III/3, III/6 and II/7 flew their aircraft to North Africa.

Chapter VI

Sand, Sand and More Sand

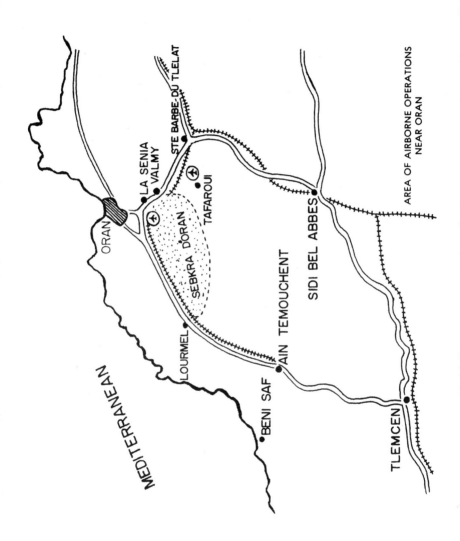

MEDITERRANEAN

ORAN

LA SENIA
VALMY
STE BARBE DU TLELAT
TAFAROUI
SEBKRA D'ORAN

LOURMEL

BENI SAF

AIN TEMOUCHENT

SIDI BEL ABBES

TLEMCEN

AREA OF AIRBORNE OPERATIONS
NEAR ORAN

59.

This encounter with the Vichy French fighters left my force with seven dead and twenty wounded. I decided to leave the dead and wounded under the care of our gallant paratroop doctor Bill Moir and to press on toward our objective.

Before the sun went down, I counted sixty men in my little task force. They were a grim and angry-looking crew. Some of them were resolved to complete the combat mission in spite of wounds. I did not try to dissuade them.

I took a careful reading on my compass. From our terrain models in London, we could place the ground picture together pretty thoroughly. We were in the Sebkra d'Oran some fifteen or twenty miles southwest of Valmy. If we could march east until we hit the Valmy-St. Barbe de Tlelat Road, we could find Tafaraoui Airdrome fairly easily. We set out in column.

The fatigue of the day's events, the long flight from England, the march across the Sebkra, the emotional strain of our baptism of fire began to tell. The North African night fell like a velvet curtain, without warning. There was no moon. Men grunted with the effort as they quickened their steps to catch up after weariness had caused them to lag behind a step or two. Every trooper was carrying some item of equipment. Men silently passed machine guns when a bearer would stumble or falter.

At the end of two hours, we halted. The troopers slumped to the ground without speaking. I called softly for a radio operator. He came padding in the darkness.

"See if you can get Colonel Raff."

The radio sputtered and hummed. There was a bullet hole through the metal case, but the operator said that he didn't think the insides were hurt. He tried for several minutes to get our command post. Perhaps they had been attacked by the enemy and destroyed, perhaps -- A faint, reedy voice came through the set. "Yarborough, this is Raff. Can you hear me?"

I answered.

"Where are you?" The voice came back.

"I can't tell you, Ed. The enemy may hear. We've had a little hard luck. We're going on into "T", do you hear Ed, we're going on to "T". Is it in our hands?"

The operator tried frantically to get an answer. Only static came from the receiver. It was so loud that I was concerned that the Arabs might hear it and report our position to the enemy. Sound carries over great distances in the desert at night.

"Switch off the receiver."

"But Sir, how about "T", we don't know whether it's occupied by us or not."

"We'll march in there and find out. That damn thing makes too much racket."

The radio operator telescoped his aerial and lay down on the sand to snatch a minute or two of rest.

Again we pushed on and rested - pushed on again and rested again. I hadn't thought there was so much sand in the world. Endlessly, it stretched before us.

At one halt, a sergeant who had been wounded in the arm had to be helped to his feet. Another paratrooper tried to take his rifle to carry it for him.

"Gimmie that gun", the sergeant growled, "I'll carry mine, you carry yours!"

Later I fell back along the column to see how things were going. The sergeant had fallen a little behind, but jogged a few steps to catch up when he saw me.

"Ok major, I'm OK," he said panting.

I wanted to help the trooper, but we couldn't halt for long. The men were too tired to support him as we walked. I trotted back to the head of the column. At the next halt, the sergeant was not to be found. He had slumped down silently in the darkness somewhere back along the trail.

The column of struggling paratroopers began to string out, try as they would to keep together. I glanced at the luminous dial of my watch. It was 0205 hours. I was numb with fatigue. I knew that the men who were carrying machine guns must be miserably tired. We halted when we reached a sandy, two-tracked road.

I told the men that they could rest for an hour. Most of them did not even hear me speak. They were asleep as soon as they touched the ground.

I directed Captain Berry to send out four riflemen to guard the sleepers. The four got slowly to their feet without a word, and vanished into the darkness.

The night was becoming bitterly cold. Our parachutists' uniforms were cotton and did not afford much in the way of warmth.

I took the liner out of my steel helmet, and used the steel part to scoop a shallow trench in the ground. It was some small protection from the chilling wind. I pulled the dried weeds from a clump near me, and placed them on my chest and body. This was a damned poor substitute for a blanket.

It seemed that I had just stopped shivering long enough to drop off to sleep for an instant when I awoke with a start. Someone was shaking my arm. I sat up trying to remember who and where I was.

"Major, there are some tanks or something down the road a piece, and I thought I better come and tell you about it."

It was the sentinel Captain Berry had sent out for security.

I shook Berry who got up like a zombie. We had been asleep for about twenty minutes.

Berry and I followed the sentinel for about a half mile. I could make out the dim outline of a clump of trees ahead and on the left.

Our guide froze in his tracks. We could hear it too. The sound of a motor drifted in a steady purr from among the shadows.

"What is it, Berry?" I asked.

"Sounds like a tank to me, major."

"It might be an enemy tank. We had better take it easy." We

left the road and walked noiselessly along on the sandy bank.

The motor sound took on a higher pitch. I could hear muffled voices among the sounds of the running engine, but I could not tell what language they were speaking.

It was a tank all right. We dropped on our stomachs as the familiar metallic clank of the tank treads became more and more distant. At least the vehicle was not headed in our direction. None of the three of us had an anti-tank grenade.

It seemed like a good idea to press on down the road a little farther. If there was an enemy tank parked nearby, we needed to know about it.

I could see dimly some large dark mounds ahead. As we approached them, a dog began to bark ferociously.

I touched Berry's arm. We stood motionless, listening to our hearts beat. A voice spoke gruffly to the dog. With a mental sigh of relief, I recognized neither French nor German. The language must be Arabic.

I walked toward the sound of the voice.

"Bon soir," I tried hopefully. No sound came from the anonymous voice, but I could hear the scuffle of footsteps approaching us. I clicked the safety catch on my carbine and waited.

An old Arab stood blinking in the beam of Berry's flashlight. His face was tanned and wrinkled by the African sun. He had a patriarchial white beard which was almost the color of his hooded burnoose.

Berry lowered his light.

I pointed to Berry, then pointed to myself.

"Friends," I said, "We are friends, *Nous sommes amis."* I knew my West Point French was a little on the weak side, but I didn't suppose all of the Arabs spoke such a good brand of French either.

"Americains," I said, *"Nous sommes Americains."*

The old man still said nothing. He motioned for us to follow him. We did so cautiously. I whispered to our paratrooper sentinel to go back and wake up the men, and to bring them up the road.

We had followed the old man but a few yards when we were joined by another younger Arab. The old man said something to him and the young man gave me a friendly slap on the shoulder.

"Americains," he said, *"C'est bon ça, nous Arabes, nous aimons beaucoup les Americains."*

The four of us sat down at the foot of one of the haystacks. I offered cigarettes to the two Arabs and they inhaled deliciously.

Bit by bit, I learned that we were not far from Valmy, and that Tafaraoui was about ten miles to the southeast. They said that tanks had passed along the road near where we were several times during the night, but that they did not know what nationality they were.

I reached down into one of my deep leg pockets and drew out a "K" ration box. I handed the waxed package to the old man. He accepted the offering without comment and began to fumble with it. I opened the box for him, and showed him how to open the can of cheese. They were both delighted with the food.

The young Arab talked of the hardships imposed upon his people by the German and Italian Armistice Commissions. He said that many Arabs could not get enough to eat and that articles of clothing were next to impossible to secure.

In a burst of patriotic expansiveness, I assured him that now that the Americans were in North Africa, no one would go hungry or without clothing.

I offered him a shirt and some woolen underwear if he would guide us to Tafaraoui. He accepted with enthusiasm.

When the column of paratroopers arrived at the haystacks, I let them rest for about ten minutes and we hit the trail again. By this time, we were so completely exhausted that we could scarcely groan. We dragged one leaden foot after the other, but not a paratrooper threw away a weapon or a round of ammunition.

We must have marched in our sleep for the next four hours.

At one point, we saw a light gleaming in the distance. Our guide told us that we were getting very near Tafaraoui Airdrome now. We had been getting "near Tafaraoui" for the last ten hours. We plodded on.

To the west, a faint tinge of daylight appeared. We would have to hurry, or Vichy airplanes might catch us still struggling along the road when dawn came.

Dead ahead, a column of shadows became trees. There was something familiar about that pattern.

Crosby was marching along at my side. He spoke in low tones.

"Isn't that the northwest end of Tafaraoui, Major sir?"

I raised my arm as a signal to halt.

"That sure as hell looks like the line of trees on our scale model. That's it all right. The barracks must be just east of those woods."

With the help of our Arab guide, we had reached the vicinity of Tafaraoui just as dawn was coming up. As we approached the northwest edge of the installation, we were sure of our target. The scale model we had studied so carefully in England had been accurate in every respect. Even in the thin morning light, an "L" shaped clump of trees told us exactly where we were.

I called for six tommy gun men and sent them ahead as a point. We moved cautiously toward the trees. Anticipation of action made us forget some of our fatigue.

The point came to a paved highway running toward the southwest. They halted and I hurried up to look the situation over. This would be the road running toward Sidi Bel Abbes and Tlemcen south of the Sebkra. We were sure of our position now.

The column of troopers moved across the road and into the ditch on the far side. It was still too dark to see any distance, but day light was not far off. I called Berry for a hasty consultation. We got down into the ditch to talk.

بطاقة تحقيق الشخصية

Name *Arthur Kellar*

Rank *Sgt. Co "E" 509th Para*

Members of the Paratroop Task Force were issued Safe Conduct Passes like the one carried by Sgt. Arthur Keller of the 509th Parachute Bn.

إلى كل عربي كريم

السلام عليكم ورحمة الله وبعد فحامل هذا الكتاب من
جيش الولايات المتحدة وهو صديق لكل الشعوب العربية
فنرجو أن تحسنوا معاملته وتحافظوا عليه من كل الأضرار
وأن تقدموا له الطعام والشراب وترشدوه إلى
أقرب معسكر أمريكي أو بريطاني وسنكافئكم
بسخاء على خدماتكم والسلام عليكم ورحمة
الله وبركاته .

FRANKLIN D. ROOSEVELT

رئيس الولايات المتحدة الأمريكية

To all Arab peoples greetings and peace be upon you. The bearer of this letter is a soldier of the United States Government and a friend of all Arabs. Treat him well, guard him from harm, give him food and drink, help him to return to the nearest American or British soldiers and you will be liberally rewarded. Peace and the mercy of God be upon you.

FRANKLIN D. ROOSEVELT,
President of the United States of America.

Messages in Arabic and English printed on the safe conduct card.

Salut a tous les Arabes, que la paix soit avec vous. Le porteur de cette lettre est un soldat du Gouvernement des Etats Unis et un ami de tous les Arabes. Traitez le bien et protégez le, donnez lui à boire et à manger, aidez le à retourner au poste Americain ou Anglais le plus proche et vous serez génereusement recompensé. Que la paix et la bénédiction de Dieu soit avec vous.

FRANKLIN D. ROOSEVELT,
President des Etats Unis.

The same message in French. This card is stamped and issued on October 1, 1942.

USEFUL WORDS	
ENGLISH	**ARABIC (phonetic)**
1. Salutation of a stranger meeting another	Salām alaïkum
2. Take me to the Americans or English and you will be rewarded	Dulnee ilal amerikāniyeen au al ingleez wa tahud feloos
3. American	Amerikānee
4. Friend	Sadeek
5. Water	Moya
6. Food	Akl
7. Money	Feloos

The rear of Sgt. Keller's card showing several important Arabic words with phonetic pronunciation.

Aerial view of Tafaroui Airdrome, south of Oran, Algeria 1942.

70.

I thought I heard the sound of an airplane motor. Berry said he had heard it too. We stopped talking.

The sound of the motors became louder and louder. It seemed as though the ship was going to pass over the very spot where we were halted.

"I hope that's one of our guys. If I never see another Dewoitine Fighter, it will be too soon."

Berry's voice was drowned out by a sudden long burst of heavy machine gun fire. The guns were not three hundred yards from where we were.

A mass of tracers streamed upward like comets, arching toward the airplane which was now dimly visible. The ship banked and dove off to the left.

"Godamighty." The voice came from behind me. "If that isn't American flak...but you know, I'm just damn near too tired to care."

There was no time to lose. This was Tafaraoui, all right, and we were going to force the issue now or never.

Across the road and about 100 yards distant, was a farmhouse with a few trees in front of it. I sent the bulk of the troopers across to take up a position facing toward the direction from which the flak had risen. Their orders were to open fire if our advance party ran into any opposition.

I put a round in the chamber of my carbine and crawled down the ditch after the advance guard.

It was getting quite light by now. A paratroop sergeant was kneeling in the ditch ahead looking along the barrel of his rifle at something across the road.

"What do you see, sergeant?"

"I'm not so sure, sir. There are some guys in those holes over there, but they aren't American and they aren't talking American."

Yes, I could see them too. In front of a group of white mud buildings was an entrenched area. Some red caps were visible in the trenches.

"I wonder why they don't fire."

"I don't know, sergeant, but this ought to swing the deal." I filled my lungs and called out the password.

"Heigh ho si-i-ilver." Then I ducked down into the ditch. Nothing happened. A little more boldly now, I poked my head above the ditch, and cautiously stood up. Still nothing moved. I climbed onto the road, holding my carbine at high port, and started toward the position.

A remarkable thing happened. The holes and trenches began to disgorge red-hatted native troops, their hands in the air.

"What the hell is this, a trap?" The sergeant eyed the group suspiciously. "Some of our guys must be here already, sergeant, let's go!"

We stepped over the fence and picked our way through the barbed wire. The native troops stood aside to let us pass.

A mud and oil-stained American armored force soldier was leaning against one of the huts rolling a cigarette. He had a two days' growth of beard on his face. A tommy gun hung from his shoulder.

He regarded us without surprise or interest.

"Any fighting here?" I asked.

"Yes sir, a little. We got about fifteen hundred prisoners around here and no place to put 'em."

He licked the paper on his cigarette and placed it in the corner of his mouth.

"Oh yes," he remembered, "The Foreign Legion is on its way up here from Sidi Bel Abbes. The Air Corps spotted them a few minutes ago just south of the field."

The Foreign Legion! And that gang could fight too. We had seen enough movies to be damned sure on that one point.

I hurried down to the air control tower. Machine gun bullets from the air had chipped great chunks from the walls. Shattered windows showed how violent the attack had been.

A group of about one hundred French sailors was lined up in front of the Operations Office. I walked in. Some of our airmen were asleep on the concrete floor. Colonel Schofield sat with his chair tilted back, and his feet on the table.

"Ah, the paratroops, I presume." I was too tired to quip back.

"How the hell about this Foreign Legion bunch?"

"Oh, it will be an hour or more before they show up. Besides, our fighters are beginning to come in."

"The Spitfires will take care of them."

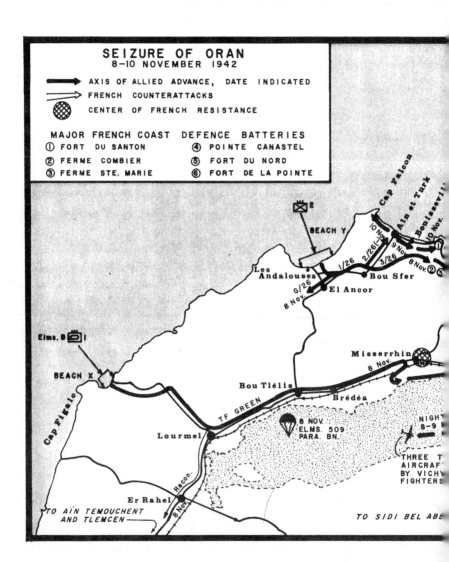

SEIZURE OF ORAN
8–10 NOVEMBER 1942

➤ AXIS OF ALLIED ADVANCE, DATE INDICATED

→ FRENCH COUNTERATTACKS

⊛ CENTER OF FRENCH RESISTANCE

MAJOR FRENCH COAST DEFENCE BATTERIES

① FORT DU SANTON ④ POINTE CANASTEL
② FERME COMBIER ⑤ FORT DU NORD
③ FERME STE. MARIE ⑥ FORT DE LA POINTE

74.

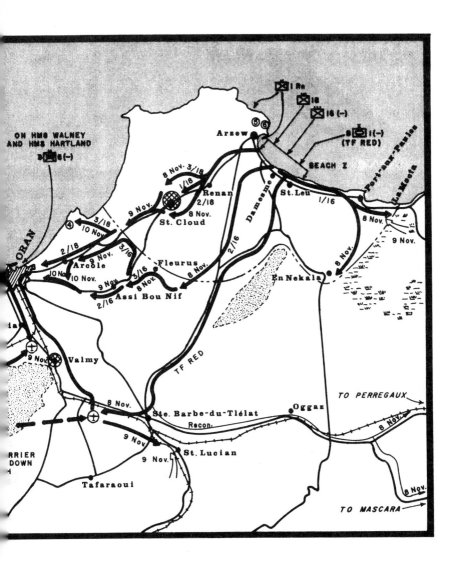

75.

Chapter VII

Tafaraoui.
Whose Flag Should Fly?

A Vichy French Naval bomber lies damaged at Tafaraoui Airdrome, November, 1942.

I had a lot of faith in Spitfires, but Tafaraoui was originally a Paratroop baby. Besides, I wasn't at all sure that the decision as to the ownership of the airdrome had already been reached with the enemy.

In front of the Operations Office, I ran into Captain Medlin. He had succeeded in sneaking a group of parachutists into the eastern end of the airdrome at dusk after we had been shot down. His troopers had guarded that end of the field throughout the night. I told him where our dead and wounded were and directed him to get help on the way.

By the time the Legion arrived within striking range, Paratroops had manned fox holes and slit trenches at a dozen points around the entire airdrome.

I could see considerable tank activity to the south. Some of the vehicles were our own light tanks, the others farther to the south were too far away to identify. I knew they were not all ours, as a considerable volume of firing was coming from that direction.

The Foreign Legion's first calling card came whistling over at about ten o'clock, and burst in an oily black puff about one hundred yards from a group of our airplanes on one of the runways.

The field exploded into activity. Ground crews ran for the shelter trenches and another then another shell burst, each one coming closer and closer to the ships. The Legion artillery was ranging in, and would soon begin its deadly "fire for effect".

Even while the shells were whistling through the air and detonating with brilliant flashes on the airdrome, a half dozen Spitfire pilots were running for their airplanes. They were in the air in seconds, it seemed, streaking toward the olive grove to the south from which the Legion battery was firing.

The Foreign Legion's artillery shells were beginning to land steadily among the planes now. Unless the Spits got there soon...

Ten or twelve light tanks burst suddenly from cover along the Oran Road and started across the open stretch toward the

Legion position. They were going as fast as they could, bouncing along like antelopes.

"Look there, major, what the hell is he going to do?" The soldier next to me in the trench was following a Spitfire with his finger. The Spit was going into a power dive toward the tanks. Down he came, closer and closer to the racing vehicles. His machine guns began to blaze. Tracers almost obscured the tanks, striking the ground around them and ricochetting off into the distance. Clouds of dust arose from the impact of the projectiles. The Spit zoomed into the blue and banked for another run at the target.

We were too astounded at this development to even talk. The tanks were American! The Spit pilot evidently didn't know the difference between our tanks and the enemy's. He was coming in for a second run at the madly racing little tanks. Again the vehicles were obscured by tracers and dust. A second Spitfire, seeing the action, approached, then a third. One by one they peeled off and rained tracers down upon the struggling vehicles.

We shouted at the top of our lungs.

"Go it, tankers, get in the woods before those bastards knock you out -- go it, tanks!"

The tanks finally made the woods, and vanished. We could not tell what casualties they had suffered, but they certainly had caught a point blank strafing.

To the south, four or five fighter airplanes were diving at something on the ground. We could see their tracers dart down, but the target was obscured from us by the intervening terrain. Our Spits headed for the scene of the action.

Presently, a huge detonation came from the direction of the Legion attack. A column of smoke and debris mushroomed into the air, and the battery which had been firing at our airfield was silent.

I was suddenly very tired. I stumbled back to the Operations Office and wandered in. One of our Allied Underground agents was there with a whole pouch full of francs. He was paying off the young Arab who had acted as our guide during the night. I was too tired to talk. I lay down on the concrete and slept.

Somehow the situation at Tafaraoui was brought under control. It was one not covered in any of the field manuals I had read. After finally agreeing to surrender, the French Garrison, predominantly Navy Air personnel, immediately put up a clamor about displaying the French flag over the bullet-riddled operations building. There was much acrimonious argument among types who a few hours before had been trying to kill each other, before it was wisely decided that both flags had to be flown -- and they were!

Ed Raff and the remainder of the Paratroop Battalion arrived later in the day of 9 November and he began immediately to get his force ready for further action.

Chutes were picked up, repacked and equipment was checked. Airplanes were repaired and maintained as well as available tools would permit.

Although I had accompanied the invasion as Executive Officer of the Paratroop Task Force, I was not actually a member of Raff's outfit. I belonged to the plans section of General Clark's staff. I knew that I should report to the Center Task Force Command Post in Oran as soon as possible.

On 10 November, I secured a truck at Tafaraoui, and accompanied by Paratroop Sergeant Carp with his tommy gun, headed for Oran about twenty-two miles distant.

The countryside looked prosperous. Mile after mile of carefully kept vineyards stretched in all directions over the rolling hills.

At one point, we passed a shattered enemy tank standing beside the road. It had burned.

Further on was a crashed Dewoitine fighter. I later heard that this was one of the Dewoitines which had caught us on the Sebkra the day before. It and one other of the three which had attacked us, were shot down by Spitfires shortly after their return toward La Senia. One of the pilots bailed out. The second was killed; the third escaped. A month later, I heard that he had joined the Boche in Tunisia, and the rumor was that he had been given a medal for putting the "Indian Sign" on us.

From the road, what we could see of the great La Senia Airdrome was a mass of ruins. The hangars had taken a terrific pasting. Commander Pugh of the Royal Navy hadn't been kidding when he had said during our planning days that he was damned well going to lay a "stick" along the hangar line if we failed to sabotage the Vichy aircraft based there.

People cheered and made the sign of the V as we rolled through the narrow streets of Oran. A Gendarme in his *kepi* cape directed us to the hotel in which General Fredendall had set up his headquarters.

When I reported to the General, he told me that my good friend Lt. Colonel George Marshal had been killed in action during the landing at Oran. George was the godfather of my first daughter. It was hard to realize that he was dead since I had seen him in London just before he sailed for Africa. We both had served as junior officers under General Fredendall (then Colonel) in the Philippine Scouts.

When I returned to Tafaraoui, I found that Raff had taken command and had the situation under fair control. The confusion incident to the occupation of the airdrome had been terrific. In spite of all precautions, some looting had taken place. The arms storeroom had been broken into, and many French rifles and machine guns disappeared before a paratroop guard was sent to remedy the situation.

Raff and I had had a bet while we were still in England, concerning a certain high tower at Tafaraoui. Our model and air photos showed it quite clearly, but our intelligence agents had failed to tell us what it was for. Raff bet me ten shillings that it was a church. I said that it was a fire house and that the tower was a place to dry hoses. We were both wrong. The tower was

509th Paratroop Surgeon Carlos "Doc" Alden, wearing the maroon beret presented to him by the Commanding General of the British 1st Airborne Division, Major General F.A.M. "Boy" Browning.

With Captain Alden is a former schoolmate, Captain Ogden Kniffen then an aide-de-camp to General Mark W. Clark.

full of coal! In other respects, we found with interest that our models and our intelligence data had been remarkably accurate.

On the second day at Tafaraoui, I awoke from my concrete floor bed, feeling as though my head were inside a glass jar. I tried to lace my boots which I had loosened for the night, and found that I could not straighten up again without considerable difficulty. As the day wore on, I felt worse and worse. I wandered around aimlessly like a sleepwalker, not having a clear idea of what I wanted to do, or even who I was. Paratroop Doctor Captain Alden slipped a thermometer under my tongue as I stumbled past him one time, and he issued a long, low whistle when he read the Plimsoll line at 103. He pointed me in the general direction of the aid station, and I stumbled in where I collapsed on a vacant army cot with my head ringing like an air raid alarm.

The aid men made me as comfortable as their limited facilities would allow. This consisted of putting a fly net over my face, and of giving me a canteen cup of hot water in which was dissolved a small packet of bouillon powder from my "K" ration. I drank a little and drifted off to sleep. Wounded were being brought in constantly. Among them there were several armored force soldiers who were terribly mangled. There were also two little Arab boys lying very pale and still. They had picked up some live hand grenades from the wreckage of our transport airplane on the Sebkra, had pulled the pins, and had held them in their hands while they exploded!

I awoke to see the serious face of a young Army chaplain bending over me. He had been talking to some of the wounded and had finally come to my bed.

"How do you feel?"

"Not very well, Father."

"Are you a Catholic?"

I answered in the negative. The young Padre produced a small black book.

"It doesn't matter," he said. "I have something here that I often read to people who are sick," He thumbed through the pages. "Would you like me to read it to you?"

"It's all right, yes, Father, go ahead and read it." I closed my eyes.

Whatever it was, my tired mind soaked it up like a sponge. A peace seemed to come over me. The Padre's voice sounded kind and honest. I forgot, for a moment, the groans of the wounded around me.

He finished reading.

"If there's anything I can get for you or do for you, please let me know."

"I will, Father, thank you." His steps echoed down the hall.

Suddenly a horrible thought struck me. Why, that must have been the last unction he was giving me. Holy H. Smoke! I feel terrible, but I'm sure as hell not dying, not without a single bullet hole to show for it.

I sat up in bed and fumbled about in my breast pocket where I had my first aid packet. I took three sulphadiazine pills and began to lace up my boots.

An orderly approached my bed.

"Where are you going, major?"

"Out. Do I look to you like I'm dying?"

"You look kind of green around the gills, sir, you better stay in bed here for a day or so."

"No soap. If I get the last rites again, I may croak sure enough."

I shuffled out the door and back to the command post at the control tower. I felt better out of the hospital atmosphere.

Already, Raff had started to move toward Tunisia. Several plane loads of chutists had taken off for Maison Blanche Airdrome near Algiers.

VOL. 72, NO. 139. ** Telephone—MAin 1234 COLUMBUS, OHIO, MOND.

ALLIES, NAZIS CLASH

U. S. Parachute Troops Do Well Under Fire
DOWN NAZIS WITH TOMMY GUNS; TALES OF HEROISM ARE TOLD

By Lowell Bennett
(I. N. S. Staff Correspondent)

WITH UNITED STATES PARA-CHUTE TROOPS, CEN-TRAL NORTH AFRICAN SEC-TOR, NOV. 16.—America's finest soldiers, the hard-bitten parachute troops, have carried out all the tasks assigned them, despite what appeared to be every element arrayed against them.

The air troopers left Great Britain in giant troop carriers.

Ohio Casualty

JOHN T. MACKALL

ALLIED FORCE HEAD-QUARTERS, NORTH AFRICA, NOV. 16.—(P)—The first American to die at this headquarters, Parachute Pvt. John T. Mackall of Wellsville, Ohio, was buried with military honors here. He was fatally wounded by a French pilot who attacked the plane carrying Mackall over Oran.

Private Mackall, 22, was drafted Jan. 27 and went overseas in June.

They flew non-stop in every kind of weather for many hours, and maintained their formation almost the entire way.

They arrived here after several attempts of both Axis and Vichy planes to intercept them, in which our troops with their tommy guns shot down two attackers for certain and believe they hit others.

The troops landed on a pre-arranged target without loss, assembled in their formations, and embarked on a most difficult 30-mile desert march toward an airdrome where they took up defensive positions and held off several armored infantry attacks until United States armored troops arrived for their relief.

According to First Lieut. Stuart G. Cutler, "the best part of the desert hike when we traded our underwear with the Arabs for water."

On three occasions the Arabs picked up hand grenades, out of curiosity, and pulled out the trigger-rings. Soon after that there was a loud noise and the Arabs disappeared, Cutler said.

"The most annoying incident, however, was when some Arabs cut one of the boys' parachute shrouds, necessitating a re-issue before we were able to go into action again," the lieutenant concluded.

Capt. William A. Medlin, jr., a highly trained member of his unit, was wounded in the legs and arms but held out for the "entire 30-mile march."

"When we arrived at the airdrome," he said, "we luckily found a large number of French 'Chowchows' (Chauchat guns) the most effective rapid fire 30-caliber machine guns and similar to the British Bren guns.

"We already had plenty of side-arms and tommy guns, but after that every man was equipped with machine guns and thousands of rounds of ammunition. I am certain we had the greatest firing power of any unit in the world.

"I can tell you that we knocked off plenty of our attackers before relieving United States columns came up," the captain said.

The commander of the parachute troops outfit is a youthful Texan, Major William P. Yarborough, whose wife, Norma, resides at Chiltoncale, Staunton.

Major Yarborough is running the

organization here until he can join up with another now stationed elsewhere, with command as lieutenant colonel.

He feels that the real hero of the whole operation was Capt. Dr. William Moir from Michigan, who although wounded in the head by shrapnel after the landing, carried out his work, operating on the men for 14 hours. I learn that

Captain Moir has been recommended for the Distinguished Service Cross.

The parachute troops are most anxious to communicate with their families as soon as possible, to tell them that everything went okay in their first action. They are ready for more—and this time against the allegedly tough German troops.

Newspaper account of one of the first combat deaths of an American paratrooper, John T. Mackall. Killed by a French fighter pilot, his memory remains as Camp Mackall near the Ft. Bragg reservation in North Carolina.

Chapter VIII

Yank Parachutes Over Youks-les-Bains

By the evening of 14 November, Raff had moved the entire Task Force two hundred and fifty miles east to the Maison Blanche Airport which serves Algiers. I was on one of the last aircraft to leave Tafaraoui.

It was dusk when we arrived. I had met Jack Thompson of the Chicago Tribune at Tafaraoui. Jack was an old friend of mine from the early days of paratrooping at Fort Benning. He wanted to come with us -- so we brought him and were happy to have him along.

At the large airfield of Maison Blanche, there was feverish activity. Allied airplanes were jam-packed into every available space. A Nazi JU 52 with the swastika on its tail, sat unevenly in front of the hangar where it had been caught a week before.

The paratroops were quartered in one of the large "Air France" hangars.

They had rigged up some cooking equipment from empty gasoline tins and other odds and ends. The chow line was forming when we arrived, and we lost no time in joining it.

Colonel Raff was in one of the little rooms at one side of the main hangar. I found him examining a map with his flashlight.

"What's the good word, Ed?"

"Oh, hello, Yarborough, you just got here in time."

Under the little colonel's finger, I could see the words "Youcks-les-Bains", on the border of Tunisia.

We were going to jump the next morning on the airfield of Youcks-les-Bains, some three hundred miles to the east and near the Tunisian border. This was stimulating news.

Raff explained, "There's a good sized landing field there, and the big shots want us to deny it to the Boche".

"How about the French?" I asked. "Are they going to be reasonable?"

"I think so. General Anderson, the British First Army Commander, has taken steps to notify the French commander in that area that we are coming."

"Is that good?' The reception at Oran was still fresh in my mind. Raff smiled a little, "It's as good as we can do. See you at planeside tomorrow at 0630 hours."

There were a lot of packed parachutes lying in a pile on the hangar floor. A man with his back toward me was examining one. He clumsily tried to put it on, and as he turned I recognized Jack Thompson.

"What the hell, Jack? You're not going to..."

Jack nodded slowly. "I've always wanted to make a jump with one of these things. Tomorrow's as good a time as any."

We tried on our chutes together, adjusted the harnesses, then carried them away to be used for pillows. I was sleepy. I was getting used to sleeping on a concrete floor. We emplaned shortly after dawn. I felt grimy and my quarter inch beard prickled.

Some of Brigadier Flavell's British paratroops who were quartered in the hanger next to ours were marching out to emplane too. I wondered vaguely what their mission was. I learned later that they were on their way to jump at Bône and that my friend and classmate, Major Chuck Billingslea, was with them. The Germans also had Bône in mind and only a fluke prevented them from getting there before the British did. The flight of JU 52 German aircraft full of *Fallschirmjaeger* turned back to their base near the Tunisian Holy City of Kairouan while in full view of the Bône Airfield and only when the British parachutes were already blossoming over the objective.

In the dawn hours of 15 November, our ships got into the air without ceremony and pointed for Tunisia. Jack Thompson squirmed in his tight harness. His face was pale under the grime and whiskers, but the set of his jaw meant that he wouldn't fail us. After two years in the paratroop game, I was beginning to be able to catch that flickering something in a man's eyes that means refusal in the door of the ship. Jack had not the slightest trace of such a look.

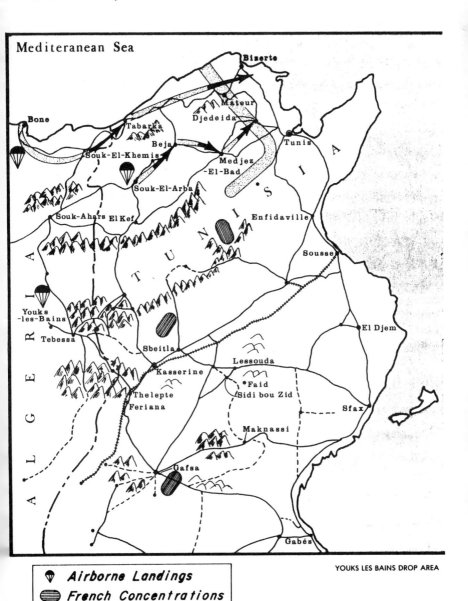

YOUKS LES BAINS DROP AREA

Legend:
- 🪂 *Airborne Landings*
- ⬗ *French Concentrations*
- ◍ *British Line*

89.

It made me feel at home to see the faces of our American paratroopers. They were young eager faces. I listened to the usual line of wise cracks many of which were directed toward Jack.

"Remember Jack, it don't mean a thing if you don't pull that string."

"Hey Sarge, ain't Jack's chute the one you caught them silk worms in?"

Jack took it like a trooper. Below us was spread a magnificent panorama of ruggedness. The jagged peaks of part of the Atlas Mountains loomed up ahead. I could pick out the tiny ribbon of road which traced its tortuous way from Algiers toward Constantine.

Soon we were among the mountains. Low hanging clouds forced our ships, at times, down into valleys while the mountain tops towered above us. At other times, we passed over peaks at such low altitudes that I felt as though I could reach out and touch their tops.

East of Ain Beida, the mountains fell away into great barren rolling plains.

When we crossed the dry bed of the Oued Mellegue, we knew that our objective was about twenty minutes away.

Through the window I could see our escort, a single Spitfire, bobbing bravely along. There was Luftwaffe in the area in strength. We were taking another hare-brained chance to fly into battle with such a minuscule amount of protection.

"Stand up!" The order rang through the cabin above the sound of the motor. "Hook up!" We snapped the metal fasteners of our parachute static lines to the overhead anchor cable.

Even after forty-one jumps, my heart beat just a little faster as I tensed my muscles for that spring into the cold blast of the slip stream. I took a turn of my carbine slung around my wrist and grasped the little weapon tightly in my left hand. The column of

90.

paratroopers was swaying to and fro with the motion of the ship as it slowed to jumping speed. "Go!"

I was moving toward the door as I had done so many times. I felt all right now -- eager to get into the air.

"Go to it, Jack," as I slapped him on the shoulder. "Out you go fella." Jack disappeared into the blast, and a split instant later I followed him. I felt the old familiar shock as my canopy opened.

Parachutes filled the air looking like graceful jellyfish -- each one with a sting. Scattered among the undulating shining white canopies were red, yellow and blue ones carrying equipment. Wave after wave of transports roared over leaving strings of pearly spawn in their wake. Where five minutes before there had been nothing but clear mountain air, there was now a snowstorm with human snowflakes.

I hit the ground with a jar. My carbine went into the mud muzzle first. Lying flat on my back I fumbled at the snap fasteners of my harness.

With a start, I realized that I was looking at an armored car on the road which bordered the field. I looked beyond it to the high plateau which dominated the terrain. There were soldiers. Many of them. I picked up my carbine and pulled the bolt open. There was a plug of mud in the barrel. The thing was useless. I took a grenade from my pocket, and unwound the safety tape which I wrapped around the handle.

Jack Thompson landed not far from me. He seemed surprised that he hadn't broken anything.

We advanced toward the high ground where the soldiers were.

Raff led the way up the slope. Our tommy gun men followed on the alert.

From the group of French soldiers, a figure detached itself and walked toward Colonel Raff. Cautiously the French commander extended his hand. Raff took it. In an instant, tension relaxed. The French surrounded us, patted us on the backs, offered to roll up our chutes and haul them to a safe place before *"les*

Arabes" got to them. We were relieved and delighted at the reception.

One company of paratroops began immediately to dig in around the airfield. The remainder set out for Tebessa, some seventeen kilometers distance where they were also to occupy another airfield.

Raff, Thompson and I piled into the French Colonel's Renault and rode into the village of Youks-les-Bains.

Over a bottle of red wine, the atmosphere grew quite friendly.

Colonel Raff presented an American flag to Colonel Berges, Commander of the French Third Zouaves. The Colonel placed the flag on the same staff with the Zouave banner, already heavy with battle honors.

Colonel Berges said that the Germans were expected at any time, and that their patrols had been seen in the vicinity, not long before our arrival.

"Now we will fight together," he announced with emotion in his voice. "My Zouaves were very sad when they thought they were going to have to fight against the Americans. Now we will turn our guns again toward the Boche. Together we will drive him from Tunisia - and from France." We drank to that.

The Colonel unfastened the famous badge of the Third Zouaves from his tunic and pinned it on Colonel Raff's parachute blouse. "From this day, our regiment is your regiment. You and your battalion are welcome at any time, wherever the *Troisieme Zouaves* may be."

Captain Chauppard-Lallier, Colonel Berges' Adjutant, removed his badge and pinned it to my parachutist's jacket.

"This," he said, "marks the beginning of a new hope for France. With America at our side, we will win freedom again for ourselves and for our families."

I looked at the badge - silver crescent bearing 3Z and surmounted by a snarling hyena. The motto in raised letters around the crescent was in French *"J'y suis - j'y reste,"* I'm here, and

Above: American troop carrier aircraft head back toward Maison Blanche Airport near Algiers after dropping the 2nd Bn., 509th Parachute Infantry on the airfield at Youks-les-Bains.

Below: Bayonet fixed, a 509th Paratrooper advances toward the French defensive positions overlooking the Youks-les-Bains Airfield.

Officers of the 3d Zouaves Regiment confer with Lt. Col. Edson D. Raff after the 509th Parachute Battalion jump on the airfield at Youks-les-Bains, Algeria.

Major Doyle Yardley and paratroop sergeant with aerial supply bundle at Youks-les-Bains.

French officer checks map with Colonel Raff and American paratroop corporal.

French trenches are at the right of the group.

here I stay!

"The Third Zouaves are fierce like hyenas in battle," said Chauppard-Lallier. "The Boche already know a little about us." The Captain spoke with authority. I had seen the battle streamers on the Zouave standard. I was proud to wear the badge of his regiment, and I so told Colonel Berges in my halting French.

Things were happening in Tebessa. French and Colonial troops of all descriptions were streaming back from Tunis, Bizerte, Sfax and Susse. Tebessa seemed to be at the crossroads of Tunisia and Algeria. French air force men in their navy blue uniforms were very much in evidence as were red hatted infantry *Tirailleurs.* There were *Spahis* in tan turbans which they called *"Shesh,"* there were *Meharists,* or camel corps men, tan and bronzed from the glare of the Sahara sun. Occasionally I saw groups of tank men whose distinctive padded steel helmets made them look as though their headgear were on backward.

All were seeking arms and equipment. Many did not believe that the Americans had landed in North Africa, until they saw us - then they were like children in their joy.

Gun emplacements began to appear around the ancient city of Tebessa. Weapons came out of hiding from under piles of camel dung. Spahis took to partrolling the roads. Let the Boche come! The French had a fine score to settle with them.

The morning of my second day at Tebessa, I heard the wail of the air raid alarm on top of the Zouave barracks. I dashed out into the cuartel to get a look at the plane. A red hatted Zouave was cranking the mournful alarm with one hand, while pulling from the ends of the multiple horns of the device, his personal equipment which he had placed there during his tour of duty as an air look-out.

The plane approached and the sound of the motors grew louder. It came into view at about 2000 feet altitude over the air-field where two companies of our parachutists had dug in. Lazily

War correspondent Jack Thompson of the Chicago Tribune newspaper. He jumped with the Paratroop Task Force at Youks-les-Bains.

Thompson was the first American civilian to jump into compat with American troops. He later jumped into France on D-Day, June 6, 1944.

the Nazi pilot banked. The morning sun shone on the undersides of the wings where the black crosses were plainly visible. The German JU 88 came out of his turn and started toward the Tebessa airfield in a long easy glide. The paratroops had one C-47 American transport on the field. This the Boche saw, and headed for. At 600 feet, certain of an easy victim, the German's machine guns began to blaze. His surprise must have been tremendous when a blast of counter-fire rose to meet him at point blank range from a score of paratroop fox holes. The German fought for altitude, his motors roaring now. A long feathery wisp of gasoline fanned into the slip stream as he dropped his plywood belly tank. He disappeared over the range of hills to the south, trailed by a plume of smoke. Arabs brought in some wreckage that afternoon. The paratroops had drawn the first blood from the "superman".

Raff was a human dynamo. He told me, "We're going right into Gafsa after the bastards."

The fact that his little force was operating without support or without certain re-supply, bothered him none at all. He wanted Nazi hides and he was going after them as fast as he could.

It was only because of a direct order from Allied Force Headquarters that the intrepid paratroop colonel was persuaded to abandon his audacious plan.

I returned to Algiers by air to report to my Chief, General Mark Clark. The General was very pleased to learn of the French attitude in the Tebessa area, and was glowing in his praise of Raff's work. He showed me a message which had come from Tebessa. Colonel Raff had comandeered transportation and had pushed over a hundred and fifty kilometers south east to Gafsa.

"I'm sending Raff some help," General Clark had said. "I think he can probably use some infantry and some tank destroyers."

I knew that Italian tanks had been reported in Sened and

Kebili, and agreed that our parachutists would shortly have need of some heavy support.

The law of compensation was quick to catch up with the Axis bandits, however. Raff's force, on its withdrawal, ran headlong into the tank destroyer unit which had been sent to re-enforce them. Together they joyfully turned again toward Gafsa, this time, loaded for bear.

Before the tank destroyers could get to Raff's force, however, a column of Italian tanks started for Gafsa. The aggressive little paratroop colonel sadly prepared to withdraw to Feriana. Before leaving Gafsa, his demolition men set fire to the gasoline supply to prevent its falling into Axis hands. That night, with the eerie light of the flaming gasoline casting long shadows ahead of them, the paratroops turned north in retreat.

When the Germans and Italians entered Gafsa, they held the French Gendarmes to the points of bayonets while Arabs ransacked the entire village, looting and pillaging.

I saw the shattered Italian tanks which had tried to prevent the Yankee reoccupation of Gafsa. I did not see the bodies of the twenty Arab looters who had faced the firing squad in the public square, and had been left there for twenty-four hours as a grim exhibit, but I gathered numerous eyewitness accounts for my report.

I joined Raff's force again at Feriana the day that the French Artillery General Welvert pinned the Legion d'honneur on the little colonel's tunic for his work at Gafsa.

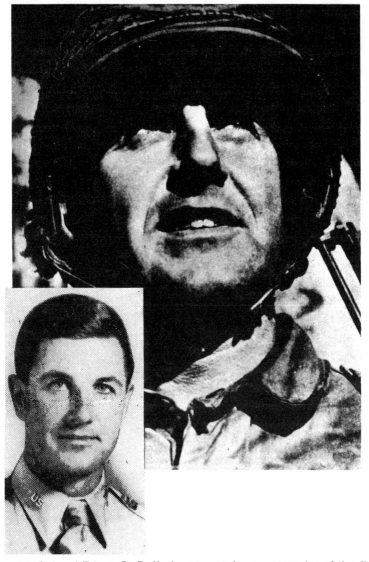

Lt. Colonel Edson D. Raff, the aggressive commander of the first American parachute assault in World War II. He later commanded a combined force in North Africa which came to be known as ''Raff's Tunisian Task Force''.

Chapter IX

Raff's Tunisian Task Force

Raff's Tunisian Task Force, as we now began to call it, was growing. In addition to the paratroops, there were now a battalion of the 26th U.S.Infantry under Lieutenant Colonel Johnny Bowen, a company of Algerian *Tirailleurs,* a British anti-mine engineer detachment, and a company of tank destroyers under Captain Ellman. This was a miniature blitz army. Raff was not the man to let it sit idle.

Our native intelligence agencies had brought numerous reports concerning a German and Italian defensive position at the Pass of Faid, a few kilometers northeast of Sidi-bou-Zid. Faid is an important terrain feature, in that it is the last actual barrier or obstacle to be crossed on the road from Tebessa to Sfax. Raff's decision to attack Faid came as no surprise to us.

On the night of November 29, he sent the light platoon of Ellman's tank destroyer company toward Faid with orders to take prisoners so that we could question them about their defenses. It was a good one hundred and eighty mile trip - Feriana to Faid and return. The light platoon got back to Feriana after daylight the next morning. It was empty handed. Its commander said that he had taken the wrong road at Lessouda and had gone into Sidi-bou-Zid. They had seen no Germans.

Again, that evening, the Little Colonel aimed the light platoon at Faid. This time he and I followed it in a jeep. We passed through Kasserine without stopping. At Sbeitla we could see dimly the outline of an almost perfectly preserved Roman Arch which stands among the Roman ruins. We stopped in Sbeitla long enough to drink a cup of date-seed coffee with some French officers whose troops were outposting the roads in that vicinity. We threaded our way through the French road blocks east of Sbeitla, and headed into German country. We turned out all lights after passing Sbeitla. Our driver felt his way along the sandy road, occasionally running off into the shallow ditch alongside.

At about 3:30 A.M., we heard the sound of motors in the distance. We quickly pulled our two jeeps off the road and hid behind some sand dunes. After a few minutes, the light platoon came abreast of our position. We hailed its commander cautiously with the familiar "Heigh Ho Silver," and emerged on-to the road.

His disappointment equalled Raff's. This time his platoon had entered the Village of Faid itself and had seen no Boche. An Arab, however, had told them that the pass just east of the village was full of them.

"It won't be full of them this time tomorrow," Raff observed ominously.

We returned to Feriana and began to prepare for the battle which was to come.

At 1730 hours on 1 December, our column cleared the road block north of Feriana, and headed toward the Faid Pass.

Our plan for attacking Faid Pass had been hastily but carefully worked out. "Mr. Charpentier", a French resident of Sidi-bou-Zid, had provided us with a very complete contour sketch of the pass and of the terrain in the vicinity. Mr. Charpentier had even agreed to accompany our assault force as a guide. We dressed him in an American uniform and gave him a rifle to carry. At least, if he were captured, he wouldn't be shot summarily as a spy in civilian clothes.

Although not designed for the purpose, the tank destroyers were to lead the assault. The plan was for them to advance upon the German position from the rear, performing the combined role of artillery and tanks. Necessity was the mother of expediency.

The French Sector Commander, General Welvert, had given us one company of the 7th Algerian *Tirailleurs*. This company was to follow the tank destroyers into the pass, deployed as skirmishers. A coordinated attack on the enemy's right flank was to be launched in conjunction with the *Tirailleurs'* assault, by our own infantry and parachutists.

From the airfield at Youks-les-Bains, where we had jumped seventeen days before, four American P-38 Lightnings were to take off in time to strafe the pass for five minutes prior to the opening of our ground attack.

The night was cold. I wrapped an army blanket around me and tried to get a little sleep as our column rumbled along. The tank destroyer half track cars made a hell of a noise. I was sure that the enemy could hear us coming for miles.

We passed Sbeitla which I recognized by the silhouette of the Roman Arch which I had seen the night before. Again we wove our way among the sandfilled trucks which had been placed as road blocks on both sides of the highway leading from Sbeitla.

It seemed hours until we again saw anything but shadowy flat terrain.

We were within a few minutes of Lessouda when our driver, who had been feeling his way along the road in absolute darkness, jammed on his brakes and pointed ahead.

"What the hell is that?"

I could barely make out a huge irregular shape on the left side of the road. We approached it cautiously, our carbines in our hands. At a range of twenty or thirty feet, I could see that the shape was a large troop-carrying lorry. The windshield was smashed and all of the tires were flat.

A hundred yards beyond the first truck, was a second, then a third. There were five of them in all. Four of them had been burned.

They were not British or French or American. Our P-38s must have caught this Axis column on its way toward Sbeitla.

We passed the ghostly burned-out hulks, and pressed on.

At Lessouda, we turned right toward Sidi-bou-Zid, which we reached in a half hour. Mr. Charpentier guided us around the village along a sandy wagon track.

"This way to Faid Pass from the rear," he said.

"Faid is fifteen kilometers to the northeast of here. By going straight east along this road, we will come to another small pass which is just about eight kilometers south of Faid. By going through this small pass, we can place ourselves between the Germans and Sfax, across their line of withdrawal."

We inched along the wagon track. Ahead of us loomed the rugged outlines of a range of rocky hills. The road was getting worse by degrees.

Raff sent Lieutenant Roworth with his British Engineers ahead of the column to look for anti-tank mines or prepared demolitions. The column halted while Roworth and his squad vanished into the darkness. They returned in about forty minutes with word that the road was clear.

"How the hell do you know, Roworth," I asked him, "you don't have any such thing as a mine detector with you, do you?"

"I smell 'em out, Major," he had replied. I think Roworth really could. He seemed to know instinctively where the Boche would or would not place mines and booby traps.

The column moved forward again, more slowly now as the road became a precipitous path. At one point where a stream crossed it, making a deep ditch, shovel men had to dig out the rear wheels of the troop-laden lorries.

Momentarily I expected the enemy to do something to hinder us. Nothing happened.

The faint light of dawn was beginning to glow by the time we had traversed the pass.

Raff ordered the vehicles to leave the column and to disperse along the eastern slope of the range of hills.

Daylight developed rapidly. I anxiously scanned the sky for German aircraft. They were usually about at dawn, and I was certain that the Boche in the pass eight kilometers north of us knew of our presence by this time.

The armored tank destroyers began to move north toward the back door to Faid Pass. Our infantry and parachutists were piling out of the trucks and were moving in small columns toward the hills, carrying their machine guns.

They were making ready for the attack on the enemy right flank.

I found Mr. Charpentier, our guide, sitting on the running board of a truck.

He was talking in staccato French to Lieutenant Roux of the French General Staff.

"Roux, let's go along with the tank destroyers," I suggested.

"I think that is a good idea."

Roux and I boarded a jeep and headed north into the dust of the half tracks.

The red ball of the sun began to climb out of the waste land to the east.

The 60th Troop Carrier Group delivers supplies for the 509th paratroopers in action in Tunisia.

105.

Chapter X

The Taste of Battle

Bedouin horsemen, at home in the hills of Tunisia, fought as light mounted infantry and gathered intelligence on enemy movements.
(Photo - Dr. Carlos C. Alden)

Our jeep turned into a cactus patch to the left of the road. The cactus was about waist high, and this particular patch was a hundred yards square.

It appeared to be a good position from which to watch the mobile artillery of the tank destroyers go into action. I could make out Faid Pass quite clearly by now. The half tracks were building up a line like pointer dogs, each with its nose toward the quarry. No firing came from the Pass. The silence was ominous. I scanned the rocks where the Boche must be lying in wait. I knew he was a cagey customer and wondered what trick he had up his sleeve -- everything so far had been too easy.

At the base of the Faid Hills, and almost in the center of the Pass was a square white mud building. The sun made it gleam. This would be a damned good aiming point.

The panorama before us seemed unreal. Distances in North Africa are deceptive, and the almost horizontal rays of the morning sun made the whole picture seem like a magnificent stage setting. It was remarkable to what extent details on objects stood out even at great ranges.

I remember a lithograph showing the panorama of the Battle of Gettysburg. To me it had looked unnatural. Here was the real thing spread out before me -- and it looked even less likely than the lithograph. Nothing had yet happened to shatter the beauty of the picture.

I heard a slight shuffle behind me, and I turned around. An Arab was approaching. He held something toward me in his right hand -- an egg. This he placed in my hand with a ceremonial gesture, and bowed his head, smiling in a friendly manner. I pointed toward the Pass, *"Le Col de Faid?"*, I asked. "Is that Faid Pass?"

The Arab nodded his head vigorously in the affirmative.

"Il y'a beaucoup de Boche la," he nodded again, signifying that the Pass was indeed full of Germans.

I dipped down into one of my voluminous leg pockets and produced a small tin of concentrated coffee. I handed it to the Arab.

"Alors, il faut que vous vous alliez," I warned, "beat it, my boy. There will be bullets flying about very shortly, and there is no need for you to be killed."

The Arab looked toward the Pass and back at me.

"Compris."

He shook hands gravely with Lieutenant Roux and me, and left in the direction from which he had come.

I looked at my watch and at the same instant, I heard the sound of airplanes approaching from the west.

These would be our P-38s, and they were hitting the time schedule right on the button.

The Lightnings came in like their namesake. A second or two after I had heard the sound of their motors, the first ship had dived shrieking into the Pass. The scene before us changed abruptly. It was a mirror-like mill pond into which a stone had been flung.

The six fifty calibre machine guns of the first P-38 began to spit simultaneously. Streams of bullets sprayed molten metal into the enemy position and bounded high into the air like flying sparks from a blacksmith's hammer.

The second P-38 dove for the Pass and vanished from view. I could hear his guns open up, their deadly staccato reverberating among the rocks with a hollow sound. A stream of tracers shot through the Pass and skipped along the ground toward the east, raising puffs of dust a mile down the road toward Sfax. On the heels of the burst, the Lightning which had hurled it ahead emerged from the Pass at an altitude of less than one hundred feet and shot into an almost vertical climb. As it banked, I could see the characteristic double fuselage of this fighter which had been designed for high altitude interception work. High altitudes! These planes were getting right down there onto the deck -- and those fifty calibers were giving the Boche hell.

109.

The German position came to life. A score of machine guns began to stutter.

The Lightnings were careening like demons around the arc of a circle, one side of which led through the Pass. The volume and intensity of their fire was unbelievable. I was glad I wasn't on the receiving end.

The armored tank destroyer half tracks were beginning to move closer to the Pass. A great geyser of dirt and debris mushroomed into the air not fifteen feet from one of the vehicles. The driver and crew made no sign that they had either seen or heard the terrific detonation. The car continued calmly toward its objective.

The burst near the half track had evidently come from an anti-tank gun on the slope just south of the Pass. Two half tracks were pointed that way now. They stood ominously silent, searching with steely eyes for the gun which had fired on them. The German gun crashed again and another flash of smoke, flame and dust bloomed this time between the two vehicles. But the tank destroyer gunners had picked up the flash among the rocks. The tank destroyer nearest us cut loose with a roar. The shell burst an instant later on the side of the hill, sending fragments of rock whining through the Pass. Number two car spoke. Another burst registered on the side of the hill. Both vehicles fired in salvo. A tremendous explosion came from the position where the anti-tank gun had been.

The vehicles were moving forward slowly now, halting to fire and then inching forward a few yards at a time. Our aircraft had spent their ammunition. They passed low over our heads and wobbled their wings to say "Good luck, ground soldiers," then headed west for the airfield at Youcks-les-Bains.

A cloud of dust was moving toward us from the direction of the spot where we had left our vehicles. As it got closer, I could see five large lorries loaded with men. The lorries stopped about three thousand yards due east of the Pass and men poured like

P-38 Lightnings provided air support for the American assault against Faid Pass 15 November 1942.

The P-38's had replaced the outclassed P-40's as U.S. aircraft production increased. However, pilots such as Major Phil Cochran in his P-40, regularly made life miserable for the Germans.

P-38 aircraft at forward assault airfield near Thelepte, Tunisia.

ants over the sides onto the ground. I could see their officers wave their arms and I could faintly hear the sound of their whistles as they formed the troops into a long skirmish line.

The line began to move toward the Pass.

Up ahead a remarkable example of coolness and pure guts was being enacted. The tank destroyer half tracks were closing in on the Pass like tigers after a water buffalo. They were firing regularly now, in perfect cadence. Number one car fired, then in order, number two, number three, and number four followed suit. The hillside and pass entrance ahead of them were at times almost hidden by the smoke and dust of the shell bursts. Each car moved like a chessman. One car moved forward twenty-five or thirty yards and halted. After it was in position, another car pulled alongside, then another, then another. Then all fired just as though they were on a gunnery exercise on the target range.

I watched fascinated, as the TD's got closer and closer to the Pass. The German fire was a steady roar now that our P-38s had gone and the Boche had come out of their dug-outs.

I could hardly believe my eyes at the coolness of those TD's. The leading vehicles were now inside the Pass itself. Murderous small arms fire was plunging into the open-topped cars from the heights above. Tank destroyer machine gunners retaliated furiously, but the Boche was hard to see and hard to hit among the rocks.

The left flank of the Algerian *Tirailleurs* was abreast of us now. Their long skirmish line pressed steadily toward the enemy. I noted the determined looks on the brown faces of those who passed close to me. The morning sun struck fire from their long skewer-like bayonets.

Lieutenant Roux was watching the Algerians. He looked at me and at the German position. I nodded.

We began to follow the Algerians.

Roux was lightly armed. He had only his pistol which he carefully removed from its holster and loaded with a click.

I had my parachutist's carbine and plenty of ammunition around my belt. In addition, I had my 45 calibre automatic and a fragmentation hand grenade.

Behind the Algerian *Tirailleurs*, Roux and I became the second wave of the attack. I looked at Roux from time to time. He was very tall and thin and his features were swarthy and angular. He had been in the Battle of France and wore the Croix de Guerre with star for his part in it. Roux was still wearing the native *"shesh,"* which he had wrapped around his head and throat during our trip to Sidi-bou-Zid the night before. The shesh stuck out in a point on the back of his head, like a hood. I could not help but smile a little, at his harmless and somewhat wistful appearance. The smile froze an instant later when the hornet-like sound of a dozen bullets followed each other in rapid succession close to us. I dropped to one knee. The Algerians ahead of us were prone and firing toward the Pass. Roux was still standing.

"Get down, you fool, you'll be hit," I shouted over the sound of the rifle fire.

"We will not be hit this far away -- except by accident," he called back. "There is a better position up there with the Algerians."

I scrambled to my feet and started forward again.

This time, I was determined to let Roux call the halt first. Hornets were buzzing past our ears with more and more regularity now. My heart jumped when I heard a sharp thud fifteen feet to my right and saw from the corner of my eye a small puff of dust leap into the air and drift lazily away.

We were a few yards from the prone Algerians now; Roux kept on walking. I was getting just a little annoyed at him by this time.

A German machine gunner cut loose with a burst of fifty. They landed a little too close to suit even the placid Roux. By mutual unspoken agreement, we broke into a run and slid onto our bellies behind a low hummock twenty-five yards to our front. We were just in time. The German gunner opened in earnest this time. Bullets thudded into the front side of our knoll with solid smacks like a muscular road worker slapping the back of his shovel on the ground. Every fourth or fifth round hit a stone and ricochetted high in the air whining like a banshee.

I was beginning to get accustomed to having my face in the gravel. It was not a pleasant feeling, but at least there was none of the stark terror which I had experienced during my baptism of fire on the Sebkra almost a month before.

After about a half hour, the fire on our knoll slackened. I looked around me cautiously. In addition to Roux and me, behind the knoll there were four or five Algerians, and two of Lieutenant Roworth's British Engineers fighting as infantry with their toy-like Sten guns. With the Britishers was one of our paratroop demolitions sergeants, carrying his Garand rifle. He had ridden a tank destroyer half track into Sidi-bou-Zid, and had gone through the pass south of Faid before dawn, looking for mines with the British Engineers. None of the three men had any business out there fighting -- they were demolitions men.

A low cry came from the *Tirailleur* next to me. I looked warily over the crest of the knoll in the direction he indicated.

My heart sank. The gallant tank destroyers were catching pure hell. At times, they were hidden from sight by the smoke and dust of bursting enemy shells. Still they fought, hurling their thunderbolts against targets which I could not see inside the Pass.

As I watched, one of the half tracks on the right flank began to move. The driver turned his vehicle neatly through one hundred and eighty degrees. The car started for the rear. When it had gone about a hundred yards, it stopped, turned right about, and facing the enemy again, sent a shell into the Pass where it burst with a flash. The car on the left flank went through the same maneuver, stopping on the same line with the first vehicle to

Signposts in North Africa in the areas where the 2nd Bn., 509th Parachute Infantry is fighting.

The black smoke in the background is from artillery fire one kilometer away near Sbeitla, Tunisia.

withdraw. In order, and without hurrying, each car executed the same movement until the whole line of vehicles was a hundred yards back of its original line.

I realized, suddenly, that I was witnessing the perfect execution of what was a most difficult operation -- a daylight withdrawal from active engagement.

There was admiration in Roux's eyes. He was kneeling, head and shoulders above the knoll, to see the movement better.

Enemy fire grew triumphantly in volume as the tank destroyers moved unhurriedly back by bounds, farther and farther to the rear.

A thousand yards from the Pass, the vehicles abandoned their leap frog tactics, and set out at full speed toward the east, along the Sfax Road. A large German gun came to life. Its bursts followed our retreating cars until they were almost out of sight to the rear.

Our position was now far from enviable. With the withdrawal of the tank destroyers, we were left without artillery. The wave of *Tirailleurs* was now the front line and we were stopped by fire from the Pass. This fire began to grow like a tropical rainstorm.

I settled down behind the knoll. It was impossible to move in any direction except straight down, as rifle and machine gun fire had us effectively boxed in. I placed the muzzle of my carbine on top of the knoll. Under my breath, I cursed the guy who had designed a sight which only went to three hundred yards. The Boche were three times that far away.

Roux was working on a *Chauchat* gun belonging to one of the *Tirailleurs*. I borrowed a pair of periscope binoculars which he had, and through them, I studied the hills of Faid. I could see very clearly a shattered cannon of some sort to the left of the pass. This must have been the one destroyed by the first tank destroyer salvo. My line of vision came to rest on the white mud building inside the Pass itself. Just beyond it and a little to the right, was a brown dirt slope with some dark palm trees showing over it. I thought I saw some movement at the base of the brown slope. I ducked my head instinctively as a single sniper's round whizzed over, then cautiously I lined my carbine sights with the point where I had seen the enemy move. I raised the barrel a little for Kentucky windage, and let fifteen rounds go. I had plenty of loaded magazines, so I put another in the carbine and fired fifteen more shots. The third magazine either brought retaliation or else the Boche made up his mind. In any case, a machine gun burst of about twenty-five kicked sand and pebbles between the collar of my jump suit and my neck. I burrowed into the gravel.

Suddenly behind me, I heard a sound that I knew well. A jeep was bounding across the flat ground toward our position from the rear. Puffs of dust were springing up all around it where bullets were landing.

There was a single occupant in the jeep, which slid to a noisy halt just to the rear of our position. The driver was a young infantry sergeant without a steel helmet.

He spotted me.

"Major, I've got a mortar here, where d'ya want it?"

I made a hasty decision. "Right here, sergeant, put it right beside me here. You can fire on that white building." I indicated the square mud house in the mouth of the Pass.

The sergeant worked rapidly, getting the mortar into firing position. We watched the first shell rise high in the air and descend faster and faster along its trajectory toward the white building. The round burst with a good-sized detonation short of the target.

"Son of a bitch," said the sergeant. "All I've got is heavy shells and they kick the base plate out every time if you don't dig it in."

He set to work putting the base plate back under the mortar tube. His second shell landed very near the target and burst with a brilliant flash. A tiny figure ran from the vicinity of the building. I tried to hit it with my carbine. The range was too great. The sergeant beamed.

117.

"What now?" he demanded. Roux was studying the hillside to the front.

"Over there, sergeant, about twenty mills to the right of the white place on those rocks, I believe there is a machine gun."

"Aye, aye, sir."

The sergeant was on his knees squinting through the mortar sight, his face wrinkled with the effort.

Without warning, a prolonged burst of machine gun fire began to drop its iron hail around us. We all hugged the ground.

The fire continued. I saw the sergeant slowly lift his face from the dirt and glance sheepishly to his left and right in hopes no one had seen him dive for the ground.

He pushed his cloth hat onto the back of his head.

"Hell," said the sergeant, "I got work to do."

He put the mortar back into position, calmly laid it on the new target, and fired until his ammunition was gone. He then threw the hot mortar tube baseplate and bipod into his jeep and took off toward the rear in a zig-zag pattern with enemy small arms fire lending wings to his departure.

We had been behind the knoll a good two hours before the first elements of our infantry battalion began to work their way up the high ground to the south of the Germans. We were still pinned down by fire, and we knew that we would continue to be until our infantry was able to occupy the Germans' attention sufficiently to allow us to move.

We relaxed and waited. The sound of rifle fire was beginning to come from among the rocks to our left front, as our infantry drove in such enemy outposts as had survived the tank destroyers artillery. By looking sharply, I could detect a group of tiny figures toiling toward the heights, carrying a machine gun, tripod and all. Presently, the gun went into action. I could pick up the sound immediately. Our machine guns seemed to fire about a third more slowly than those of the Germans. Our riflemen began to build up on the line established by the machine gun. As we had suspected, the German fire on our position began to slacken.

Roux looked to me with eyebrows arched like question marks.

"OK Roux, let's get cooking!" We sprang to our feet and ran toward the hills of Faid, falling prone every forty or fifty yards, to rest and to avoid being hit.

Bullets were falling sporadically among the rocks as we climbed. By contrast, we felt safe and secure, when we were finally high enough to look down on the knoll behind which we had spent two anxious hours.

"Godamighty, they were looking right down our throats!"

Roux nodded. "Plunging fire," he said, "is difficult to adjust --so, we are still alive."

American infantry swarmed up the heights, paratroopers among them, fighting where they would do the most good.

I reached the crest of the rocky hill and looked warily down into the German position. I could see the brown slope with the palm trees on it, much more clearly now. There were some fox holes at its base, and a trench zig-zagged around its forward edge.

There was a mortar near me. Its gunner was watching me inspect the Boche position.

"See any, Major?"

"No, I can't, but I can see their fox holes."

"Well, sir, watch the bastards run now."

He loaded a round into the mortar, and ducked as it blew from the muzzle. I watched it arc into the air and burst on the top of the brown slope.

As the gunner predicted, the ensuing blast brought two little figures from their fox holes. They ran madly for the trench as our riflemen fired furiously in their wake. I didn't blame the "bastards" for coming out from under that mortar fire. I added my nickel's worth by firing fifteen more rounds with my M-1 carbine.

Two of our machine guns converged on the Boche's hiding place and opened up. It seemed that they fired for minutes without ceasing. The rocks in and around the hollow were pulverized. When the dust cleared, a booted leg slid slowly from the shadows under the rock, then remained motionless. The German gun was silent.

In the meantime, sporadic but effective fire came from a score of similar pockets among the rocks. One of our wounded was lying full length on the rocks ten feet from me. His hat was over his eyes to shield them from the sun. He was stripped to the waist and I could see a small round hole in the left side of his abdomen. I looked at his face for any sign of pain. There was none. For him, the small morphine ampoule had been a blessing. He didn't even wince when a medic with a red cross brassard on his arm came clambering over the rocks, and carefully inserted a long probe into the wound in search of the bullet.

A new note was injected into the fighting, when a loud report from the Pass announced the launching of an artillery shell in our direction. I heard the characteristic swish-ish-ish as the projectile travelled over our heads. It burst with a muffled roar among the rocks a good thousand yards to our rear.

The next round smashed point blank against the face of the rocky slope to my left upon which one of our machine guns had been placed. For a sickening instant, I saw the bodies of two men hurled into the air about eight feet, then fall among the rocks amid a shower of stone fragments and debris.

We braced ourselves for an artillery barrage. Another burst landed far to our right harmlessly. The Boche would not be able to hit us where we were, with anything but high trajectory mortars.

Some of the men were sleeping on the bare jagged rocks. They were exhausted, and the strain was beginning to tell.

Roux and I sat down under cover, and shared a "K" ration.

As we ate, I glanced toward the crest of a rise in the rocks about a hundred yards to our front. There, perfectly silhouetted against the skyline, in exactly the manner we had always taught our troops not to do, was an American soldier. He raised himself cautiously on his hands, and began to move over the hill. His path of advance was directly up a rocky draw which German machine gun fire had been sweeping most of the afternoon. One of the tired soldiers resting on the rocks near me cupped his hands and shouted.

"Hey, you dumb jerk, get away from that draw. Machine guns are firing down there." The second figure continued to advance behind the first. He carried the tripod for the machine gun. Both soldiers were now toiling up the deadly draw, with tired steps. A third figure appeared on the crest, then a fourth and a fifth. A chorus of voices sang out from our hill.

"Hey you crazy bastards, get outa that draw before the Jerries blast you out!"

The last ammunition carrier who had come over the crest following the leader with the gun on his shoulder, waited patiently for the shouting on the hill to subside.

"Aw, blow it out your bum," he called wearily.

The sound of laughter rippled through the rocks. The men appreciated this kind of humor. The little procession proceeded up the draw and put its gun into action without benefit of further advice from our hill.

The sun was beginning to sink into the Tebessa Mountains to the west, and still the Boche were biting back hard. It looked as though we would have to continue the job throughout the night and into the next day.

I was so tired that even the gunfire could not keep my eyes from drooping.

Roux and I began to pick our way out of the hills in search of Raff's Command Post. Halfway down the slope, I met Sergeant Jack Pogue, our paratroop communications expert.

"Where's the Colonel, Pogue?"

"I was going to ask you, Major; I don't know. He may be down in that cactus patch where those trucks are."

We headed toward the cactus patch. An occasional bullet sang past us when we got onto level ground again, but we were getting too far away from the Pass by now to be good targets --and I personally was getting too tired to be alarmed by anything less than the prospect of immediate annihilation.

I found the Little Colonel pacing to and fro among the cactus and looking anxiously toward the Pass.

"How's it going up there?"

"Not so good, Ed; we can't move another inch nearer, and we can't run them out from where they are."

Raff called for his jeep.

"Hop in," he said, "We're going back to Sidi-bou Zid. I'm going to call Feriana and have another company of parachutists come up tonight."

Nightfall was not far off when we got to Sidi-bou-Zid. At the Gendarmerie, I asked where the telephone center was. The captain of Gendarmes told me that the *Bureau des Postes* where the switchboard of the village was located, was down the road a couple hundred yards. I could still hear the sound of gunfire coming from the pass as I plodded wearily in search of the central.

The *Bureau des Postes* was closed and shuttered. The postmaster opened the door cautiously in response to my hammering with the butt of my carbine.

"Vous avez un telephone içi?" I inquired.

He said that he had a telephone, all right, and he raised a finger and beckoned me to follow him.

He led me into the switchboard room.

"Regardez," he said shaking his head, "see what the Italian *cochons* have done," The switchboard had been completely cleaned of the plug-in cords.

"The day before yesterday," he told me, " an Italian captain and a German lieutenant came in here and took all the plugs away. The telephones in the village are useless."

My morale dropped. I was faced with the possiblity of haveing to go all the way back to Sbeitla or even to Kasserine in order to telephone my report into Allied Force Headquarters in Algiers.

The postmaster observed the look of dejection on my face, and gave me a sly wink.

"But come with me, *mon commandant*. I have one telephone which the Italian captain did not see, and which does not pass through the switchboard."

I felt a great weight removed from my mind. We found the telephone in the outer office, hidden in the shadow of a post, and after the usual animated procedure characteristic of French telephone operations, I heard the faint voice of Colonel Dickson, the Allied Force Intelligence Officer speaking from Algiers.

I walked back to the Gendarmerie. In the courtyard there was a horse-watering trough. I washed some of the dust from my face and hands, and sat down to rest a little.

The wife of the Captain of Gendarmes sent her small son out to ask me to have a cup of hot coffee with the family.

The coffee was the usual date seed concoction, but it tasted good. I must have looked extremely tired.

The Gendarme Captain showed me a bed in one of the rooms, and told me that I was welcome to lie down if I wanted to. I accepted his invitation. I was fast asleep, fully clothed and with my web harness still on, when Roux came in five minutes later to tell me that Raff had called for Parachute Company "E" and that it was on its way to Sidi-bou-Zid.

Chapter XI

Victory at Faid Pass

A member of the 2nd Bn., 509th Parachute Infantry and four Arabs stand near a knocked-out German personnel carrier.

Left - a member of the 2nd Bn., 509th. An Arab boy holds his M-1 Garrand; Right - Sgt. Lloyd K. "Mother" Bjelland, 2nd Bn. 509th Parachute Infantry, in North Africa.

The paratroops arrived by truck about midnight. They stopped in Sidi-bou-Zid only long enough to get instructions from Raff, then they headed for Faid Pass. Their mission was to work their way onto the high ground to the north of Faid, and from positions to the east of the enemy, to attack him by fire and movement.

While I had been asleep, a battery of French seventy-five millimeter cannons had arrived from Sbeitla. It had gone into position on the edge of the town of Faid itself, and was preparing to shell the German fox holes at dawn. From Sbeitla also, a company of coal-black Senegalese troops had arrived. These were to reinforce infantry and the *Tirailleurs* for a concerted attack the next day.

I heard the French artillery battery open up at dawn. Roux and I, after a hasty breakfast of eggs fried in olive oil, headed back toward the battle. By the sound of the firing, it seemed to be raging with renewed vigor after a night's rest.

We followed the route which we had used to move to our first attack positions. When we came to the small pass which our vehicles had had such a difficult time traversing, I found that a medical aid station had been set up and was functioning. A dozen wounded were lined up on stretchers near a stream, waiting for the busy surgeon to get to them. On the east side of the Pass, I found Captain Ellman, of the tank destroyers. His face was grave as he told me how many casualties his little unit had suffered.

The night before, his light platoon had outposted the German route of withdrawal toward Sfax just in case any of the defenders of Faid Pass decided to make a get-away during the night. One of his cars had rolled up to a group of soldiers who were busily working on something in the road. The car commander evidently thought the troops were our own, and he didn't fire on them. They turned out to be Boche and Italians putting antitank mines in the road. Ellman's patrol found the empty car the next morning. The guns were still on it. The blankets of the crew seemed to be the only things missing - except for the crew itself, which were all taken prisoners except one who had escaped with the story.

The French artillery battery in front of the Faid was firing again. From a position near the cactus patch where I had started the battle the previous day, I watched the shelling. Occasionally, a round came clear through the pass and out into the open where it bounced along like a flying fish, finally exploding in a puff of black smoke. I could hear the sound of heavy small arms fire above the roar of the bursting artillery shells.

I wanted to see that French Artillery Battery in action. We moved back toward the road where our aid station was, and having traversed the Pass, turned north toward the Village of Faid.

General Welvert, the French sector commander, was in Faid personally directing the artillery fire. Paratroop Sergeant Jack Pogue was watching the shells burst in the Pass. He was visibly worried about something. Occasionally he would shake his head disgustedly as a round would kick a column of smoke and stones into the air. Finally he could stand it no longer. He approached General Welvert. The general lowered his field glasses.

"Yes, sergeant?"

Pogue pointed toward the high ground where the shells were landing.

"Sir, our troops are up there. It looks to me like you're landing the shells right among 'em."

The general handed Pogue the field glasses.

"My son," he said. "The gunners know exactly where those shells are going."

Pogue took the glasses. The general knew what he was talking about. This was beautiful shooting.

"To a Frenchman, the seventy-five is what the rifle is to the American," said Welvert with a Gallic shrug of his shoulders.

A French officer approached the gun position and said something to Roux.

"There are two German prisioners under guard in a building over there. Would you like to talk to them, major?"

I told Roux that I would like to see them. A French *poilu* marched them out. They were covered with dust and looked as though they hadn't slept for some time. One of them couldn't have been more than seventeen years old. Through an interpreter, I learned that they were Panzer engineers, and that the force holding the Pass was a composite company consisting of both Germans and Italians in the ratio of one German to two Italians. The Germans, they said, were present to see that the Italians kept fighting. I asked point blank what they thought of the Italians. The younger German soldier replied with a pantomime of a machine gunner sternly firing with head erect, eyes to the front. He then tapped himself on the chest and said "German." Next he covered his face with his hands and peeped cautiously between his fingers, wincing as though he were in mortal terror of everything he saw. "Italian," he announced. This made the French soldiers laugh and nod their heads in agreement. I searched through the German's papers, and found several printed pieces of propaganda. One was a long list of reasons why the soldiers of the Third Reich were the best in the world. Another was a typewritten copy of the words to "Deutchland Uber Alles." They told me that their food was good and adequate. One packsack had a round orange-colored plastic box which contained fresh butter. We had no butter ourselves. Their clothing and equipment, with the exception of the shoes which had cloth tops, were good and well made. Obviously Germany was not yet feeling the pinch of lack of war material.

The afternoon wore on. Raff had called for a general attack at 1730 hours. In this attack, all infantry and paratroop elements were to close with the enemy after the artillery had laid a half-hour barrage. Four armored half-track tank destroyers were to lead the attack through the Pass itself. Already they were rumbling into position near the Village of Faid.

I saw Captain Ellman in his command half-track and walked over to talk to him.

I remarked that I couldn't understand why the Germans hadn't tried to relieve their beleaguered force in the Pass either by air attack against us or by a mechanized attack from Sfax. Ellman told me in a matter-of-fact way that the Boche had indeed tried to relieve the siege of the Pass by sending a mechanized column from Sfax. He said that his tank destroyer gunners had spotted that column three thousand yards away, and had blasted the leading three vehicles. The other turned and fled.

"Do you mean to tell me that your gunners hit those vehicles three thousand yards away?" I asked.

"Sure did," he replied, "Our sights only go to 1500 yards, but my boys can aim by guess and by God."

As zero hour approached, the firing in the Pass rose to a crescendo. The *soixante quinze* battery was firing shrapnel now, which burst above the German entrenchments and rained death down into the fox holes. It was hard to see how any human being could live through that hell. The Germans must have had the same question in mind. At 1715 hours, a quarter of an hour before our all-out attack was to begin, a white flag was raised. The Boche was throwing in the sponge.

It was dusk before the column of prisoners, 130 of them, began to move out of the pass toward Faid Village. To the Senegalese fell the job of guarding them.

It seemed strange to be walking so boldly into the Pass which had been such a raging inferno a few hours before. I could hear the shouts of the Senegalese as they jabbed their bayonets toward the frightened Boche and Italians. The Senegalese were slow to anger, but once their ire was aroused, they were formidable. The Germans and Italians were visibly uneasy over the prospect of being turned over to the fierce blacks for disposition.

I saw a German helmet lying on the ground, and stopped to pick it up. Then I remembered the nasty Boche booby trap habit. I left the helmet where it lay, and walked to the top of the brown slope with the palm trees on it, at which I had fired the first day of the battle.

General Welvert's car was there. A German lieutenant looking sullen and red-eyed was sitting in it.

Darkness was falling fast. I turned back toward Faid. The prisoners had been marched into the village square and were sitting on the ground. There was a ring of Senegalese around them. I noticed that the Germans sat apart from the Italians. The Italians were talking and laughing. They appeared to be very relieved to be out of the Pass. One Italian motioned for me to come over to him. I stepped past the line of sentries to hear what he had to say.

In a mixture of French, Italian and sign language, he asked me if his wife and *bambini* would know where he was. I told him yes, that the Red Cross would send his name in as having been captured. He smiled happily at this, showing a white set of teeth.

"You know Fiorello La Guardia?" he asked.

I nodded my head. I knew of Mayor La Guardia of New York, of course. Who didn't?

"Good man," the Italian said. He laughed again.

Before long, the Senegalese were carrying water to the prisoners. A French soldier brought a steel helmet full of pocket knives for my inspection. He had taken them from the prisoners, and wanted to know if I wanted one of them. I chose one with a corkscrew. In this land of wine-instead-of-water, I had been needing a corkscrew for some time.

It was pitch black by now. I went back to Sidi-bou-Zid and rented a bed in the Arab hotel. Sleep would be delicious. The task of Faid was nearly complete.

130.

Drawing by Eleanor Meany

The regimental badge of the 3d Zouaves of the French Army. The silver device features a snarling hyena surmounting a crescent which bears the motto "J'y Suis, J'y Reste," "I am here and here I stay."

Presented to the members of the 509th Parachute Infantry Battalion by the commanding officer of the 3d Zouaves at Youks-les-Bains, Algeria on 15 November 1942, the badge was approved for perpetual wear by the 509th by Headquarters, North African Theater of Operations.

131.

Chapter XII

Incident at Lessouda

The author, (bareheaded), General Mark Clark's liasion officer
with the advanced American forces in Tunisia, questions two
German prisoners for possible information valuable to the Allied
cause. French soldiers in the background look on.

Major Yarborough wears the red fourragere of the
3rd Zouave Regiment on his left shoulder.

The people of Sidi-bou-Zid were jubilant over the defeat of the Boche. But the Germans were not going to let us have the Pass without further argument. Seven JU 88 airplanes bearing the black crosses of the Luftwaffe on their wings, appeared from the direction of Kairouan at dawn the next morning. They bombed and strafed our positions for a half hour. I had been riding with Jack Thompson and Harrison Roberts in a civilian car toward the Pass from the direction of Lessouda when the planes arrived. I saw their approach from our right rear and shouted a warning. The French driver, Jean Ruteau, jammed on the brakes, and we spilled out of the car. The planes were over us before we could get seventy-five feet away from the car.

We were not the only ones on the road. A French ambulance full of enemy wounded had just passed us on its way to Sidi-bou-Zid when the blow struck. It was now halted about fifty yards down the road and the Algerian driver instead of running for cover and leaving the wounded locked inside, was fumbling with his key at the rear door lock.

The German aircraft were banking steeply for a run at their quarry. The guns began to blaze. Little puffs of dust jumped into the air off the road and swept rapidly toward the ambulance driver. He crumpled in his tracks and lay still. The windshield of the ambulance was shattered. Holes appeared in the red cross painted on the side of the vehicle. The Boche pilot couldn't have helped seeing the huge red crosses. The last Nazi ship swept over us, his guns hurling streams of fire ahead of him.

The planes vanished as quickly as they had come. They were over the Pass again giving our troops hell.

I got up from the ground. I was shaking a little, more from anger than from fear.

Our car was a mass of flames. I had had a drum of German machine gun bullets in the car. I had intended to take them back to Algiers for our ordnance officers to look at. The heat of the burning car began to explode the bullets. Pieces of metal shell casing were flying in all directions.

I approached the ambulance. A thin wisp of smoke was beginning to curl upward from under the hood. I thought I had better look inside to see if there was anyone still alive in there after the murderous assault.

I tried to open the back door but it was locked. The dead driver probably had the key on him, but he was practically cut in half by the Boche machine gun fire. I did not feel like turning him over to look for the keys.

A faint, pitiful sound came from inside the ambulance.

"Kamerad, kamerad!"

I crawled into the front seat after looking hastily around for the airplanes which were still in the vicinity.

A German soldier strapped into a stretcher close to the ceiling of the ambulance looked at me pleadingly. His face was white with pain. A fresh wound in his forehead stood out bright red against the pallor of his skin.

"Kamerad," he moaned. He said something in German which I did not understand. Boche or no Boche, I felt sorry for him. He had lain strapped to his stretcher helpless, while his countrymen had poured lead into the ambulance. The wound in his head was a present from the Third Reich.

More smoke was coming from the motor. I was going to have to work fast.

I raised my carbine. A look of terror came into the young German's eyes. He probably thought I was going to finish him off.

I fired five rounds through the rear door lock, then I climbed out of the front seat and walked around to the rear of the vehicle. Stepping over the dead driver, I tugged at the doors until they came open.

When the air attack came, prisoners were still being evacuated from the Village of Faid. Some of them, like the ones in the ambulance, had been caught on the road. Now they were all over the landscape. I shouted at one who was limping in the

German soldiers wounded at Faid Pass are removed by German prisoners after the French ambulance in which they were being evacuated was attacked by JU-88 aircraft of the Luftwaffe.

direction of Faid.

He turned around and came toward me. Two Italians who had run from the attack voluntarily came back to the ambulance. I told the three of them to take the wounded man from the vehicle and to lay him alongside the road. The prisoner who limped was a German. In the strongest language I could think of, I told him what kind of sportsmen Nazi airmen were. I think he got the drift.

The wounded German was feeling deathly ill. The wound on his forehead was bleeding. I gave one of the Italians my first aid packet and told him to bandage the soldier's head.

We hopped a ride back into Sidi-bou-Zid, on a French truck which came out of Faid after the planes had gone home.

Wounded from the air attacks were drifting into Sidi-bou-Zid. There was one paratrooper limping along with a blood-soaked bandage around his knee. He told me that the paratroop position in the Pass had caught hell four times in a row.

In the Gendarmerie there was another German prisoner who had been rounded up after the air assault. He was waiting to be sent to Tebessa with the others. I studied the man closely. He was about thirty years of age. He had blue eyes and blonde hair. Not a bad looking man. His face was grave and serious. The expression in his eyes was one of unutterable weariness. This was a Nazi. I had thought Nazis must surely have horns and forked tails. To look at him, he might have been somebody's brother from Milwaukee.

The German talked quite freely, as he sat munching on a piece of rye bread which he had taken from his pack sack. He recognized my paratroop battle dress, and told me that his brother was *fallschirmjaeger* (paratrooper) in Crete. He said that he had already fought in Russia for a year. He had been wounded, and sent to Tunisia for a "rest".

I asked him what the German people thought about the war. He answered frankly, that opinion now in Germany was divided.

137.

At least half the people could no longer see any hope for victory.

"But Germany will continue to fight," he said, "There's nothing else for her to do."

I went in search of Raff. He was beginning to get worried about supplies. The tank destroyers were practically down on their uppers. Food, ammunition, and gasoline were low. He told me to go to Tebessa and to Algiers if necessary, and see what I could do about the situation. I left that night. Faid was in good hands. The sprinkling of paratroops throughout the action had given an account of themselves which the enemy would remember.

At Tebessa, I spent the night with "my regiment", the *Troisieme Zouaves*. Early the next morning, I boarded a transport airplane at Youcks-les-Bains, and headed for Algiers and my niche in Allied Force Headquarters to await General Mark Clark's directions. These would lead me back to the United States and an assignment which would soon return me to North Africa as a paratroop battalion commander. Ahead lay Sicily, Salerno, Anzio and the Champagne Campaign.

Feb. 2, 1943.   W. P. YARBOROUGH   Des. 134,963

PARACHUTIST'S BADGE

Filed June 19, 1942

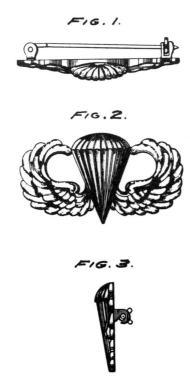

FIG. 1.

FIG. 2.

FIG. 3.

Illustrated is the final design for the parachutist badge which was designed and patented by the author.

PHOTOGRAPHS

AND

APPENDICES

Editor's Note: There may be some confusion as to the numerical designation of the unit which features in the events this book describes.

Orders from the United States, changing the units designation from the 2nd Bn., 503rd Parachute Infantry to the 2nd. Bn., 509th Parachute Infantry did not reach England until after the unit had embarked on its mission to North Africa.

These orders were brought to the unit by the rear echelon which arrived by ship in North Africa under the command of Capt. Bill Dudley. Later, in Italy, the 2nd. Bn. designation was dropped and the unit was known as the 509th Parachute Infantry Battalion.

Members of the Parachute Scout Co., 2nd Bn. 509th Parachute Infantry, commanded by Capt. Charles C. W. Howland.

The Parachute Scout Company of the 509th was the actual forerunner of the Pathfinder detachments which were later formed in the U. S. Army.

U. S. Army Photograph

143.

Members of Hq and Hq Co., 2nd Bn., 509th Parachute Infantry, commanded by Capt. Ralph H. Whitmore, Jr. in formation at Camp Kunkle, Les Angades Airfield, French Morocco.

U. S. Army Photograph

Members of the Service Company, 509th Parachute Infantry, stand in parade formation in Camp Kunkle, Los Angades Airfield, French Morocco. Service Company was commanded by Capt. Edmund J. Tomasik.

U. S. Army Photograph

Members of Co. "D", 2nd. Bn., 509th Parachute Infantry, commanded by Casper E. Curtis. Photo taken at Oujda, North Africa.
U. S. Army Photograph

Members of Co. "E", 2nd Bn., 509th Parachute Bn. at Oujda, North Africa, commanded by Capt. Archie Birkner.

147.

Members of Co. "F", 2nd Bn., 509th Infantry at Oujda, North Africa, commanded by Capt. Erven E. Boettner.

U. S. Army Photograph

Appendix "A"
C O N F I D E N T I A L

HEADQUARTERS PARATROOP FORCE
A.P.O. 650 U.S.A.

November 18, 1942

SUBJECT: Commendation.

TO: ALL PERSONNEL, THE PARATROOP FORCE

1. This force was called upon to perform a long range Parachute Mission, at night, over water, into unknown enemy territory, without meteroligical data or pursuit protection, in unarmed transports which of necessity had to be flown in an overloaded condition to accomplish the extreme range required for the mission. Celestial navigation was impossible during the first half of the flights due to unfavorable weather cnnditions and prearranged radio aids did not function properly and were of no material aid.

1. French ground and air resistance prevented the PARATROOP FORCE from dropping Paratroops on La Senia or Tafaroui Airdromes, but the presence of such a large force of twin engine Aircraft in the vicinity caused confusion among the French which resulted in their remaining on the defensive in the vicinity of their bases. Our sea convoys and our ground forces met little or no aerial opposition from Enemy Aircraft.

3. In parting from the PARATROOP FORCE I wish to commend every member of the command for his devotion to duty and individual effort on the mission. I know that I speak for every man of this command when I say "Our hearts bleed for those who were lost on the Mission."

4. It is requested that a copy of this commendation be placed on the records of all concerned.

s/WILLIAM C. BENTLEY
t/WILLIAM C. BENTLEY
Colonel, Commanding

A CERTIFIED TRUE COPY:

RALPH H. WHITMORE, JR.
Captain, Infantry
Adjutant
149.

Appendix "B"

HQ FORCE 141
B. N. A. F.
6 June 43.

From: Major General F. A. M. Browning
Airborne Troops Commander

Dear Yardley:

Thank you very much for your letter of the 29th May. I was very surprised to hear from Captain Alden that you were not aware that two months ago we asked Colonel Raff to let you know, when he passed through North Africa on his way home, that we had made your Battalion honorary members of the British Airborne Forces. However, I am delighted to confirm that you, your Officers and Men are honorary members and we are privileged and happy to know that you accept and are pleased to do so.

We are always looked upon 2nd Bn 509th Parachute Regiment as part of us and General Hopkinson is issuing an order in the 1st Airborne Division telling the news.

With regards to Berets, I have to tell you that we are so short of them owing to fitting out our Middle East Bridge that you will have to wait temporarily till we can get some more, but we are making every effort to do so.

I shall be honored to come and inspect your Battalion and if you agree, I suggest the morning of Wednesday, 15th June. I shall much look forward to seeing you again and meeting you all. I shall be very interested to see your improved organization and I hope to obtain more hints for our mutual improvement.

Hoping to see you on the 15th June.

Yours Sincerely,

s/F. A. M. Browning
t/F. A. M. Browning
Major General
Airborne Troops Commander

To: Doyle R.Yardley
Lt. Col., 509th Prcht. Inf.
Commanding   150.
APO #464, U. S. Army.

Appendix "C"

— ORDER —

The General Commander in Chief decides that the wearing of the Insignia of the 3rd Zouaves Regiment be granted as a special honour to the officers and enlisted personnel of the 2nd Bn of the 503rd Parachute Regiment of the American Army as souvenir of the 15th November and the days following, during which this Battalion cooperated with the 3rd Zouaves Regt. in the defense of YOUKS les BAINS (Department of Constantine).

This decision confirms the symbolic gesture made in the field on that date by the Colonel Commanding the 3rd Zouaves Regiment at YOUKS les BAINS when he personally pinned the insignia of his regiment on the breast of the Colonel commanding the 2nd Battalion of the 503rd Parachute Regt. of the American Army, by which action was expressed his wish to render homage to the worthy cooperation of American arms in the common struggle which was taking place.

General of Army GIRAUD
Commander in Chief

Distribution

Lt. Col. commanding 2nd Bn., 503rd Parachute Regt.
or American Army

Colonel commanding the 3rd Zouaves Regt.

Appendix "D"

FLIGHT MANIFESTS
FOR THE
NORTH AFRICAN INVASION

Author's Note: The flight manifests which appear on the following pages were copied from the originals which contain a number of errors and omissions.

For example, the name of Colonel William C. Bentley, the Paratroop Task Force Commander, does not appear on any of the lists.

Lt. Colonel Edson D. Raff, the 509th Parachute Infantry Battalion Commander is incorrectly listed as being aboard the same aircraft as the author.

There are several names spelled incorrectly and some serial numbers have been omitted. The vital necessity of meticulous care in the keeping of wartime personnel records, would become especially clear in the years following the return of the veteran troopers to civilian life.

Note: Plane Number 3 Headquarters Company, Plane Number 7 - Company "D" did not have the personnel assigned to them listed on the government manifest, hence they are not included in the sequence.

Plane Number 1 - Headquarters Company

Personel Loading	S/N	Hometown	Wt. Fully Equipped
1. Lt. Col. Edsen D. Raff	O-19261	New York, New York	271
2. Cpl. Harold A. Bachman	35166933	Elkhart, Indiana	262
3. Pvt. Franklin W. Wolfe	35130651	Cincinnati, Ohio	266
4. Cpl. Clyde W. Scarborough	6921824	Anniston, Alabama	243
5. Capt. William J. Schloth	O-339137		284
6.			270
7. S/Sgt. Jack Pogue	885620	Moriarity, New Mexico	252
8. T/Sgt. Ellis L. Bishop	35165286	Ft. Wayne, Indiana	255
9. T-5 Aureliano S. Valdez		ElPaso, Texas	245
10. T-5 John Hayes	33075831	Perkiomemville, Pennsy.	257
11. S/Sgt. Cyrus C. Paks	35129768	Berea, Kentucky	275
12. Marshall R. Savell	34151596	Fisher Louisiana	255
13. S/Sgt. Alain Joseph		New York, New York	320
14. Maj. William P. Yarborough	O-20362		

Total Weight	3725
Equipment Bundle Weight	250
Special Equipment	45
Total Weight used for Tactical Mission	4020

Plane Number 2 - Headquarters Company

Personel Loading	S/N	Hometown	Wt. Fully Equipped
1. Capt. William A. Medlin	O-323684	Florence, S.C.	270
2. 1/Sgt. Jim Swain	6392329	Troy, Alabama	250
3. Pfc. Charles A. Audet	31025044	Fitchburg, Massachusetts	245
4. Sgt. John L. Billingsley	7080551	Athens, Alabama	255
5. Pvt. Albert A. Beauchesne	20112408	Webster, Massachusetts	250
6. Pvt. Leo W. Martin	31044945	Lewistiwn, Me.	250
7. Pvt. Ralph Marez	6897807	Philadelphia, Penna.	255
8. Pvt. Curtis C. Williams	34109464	Birmingham, Ala.	255
9. Pvt. Thomas L. Silas, Jr.	34052658	Jacksonville, Fla.	245
10. Cpl. Romaine W. Hutchings	35029219	Akron, Ohio	260
11. T-5 Ernest Boudoin	34079216	Kaplan, Louisiana	260
12. Cpl. William W. Sullivan	6918198	Galesburg, Illinois	260
13. Sgt. Janes W. Collins	15063705	Williamstown, Kentucky	260
14. Lt. John R. Martin	O-399024	Eagle Pass, Texas	250

Total Weight	3565
Equipment Bundle Weight	250
Special Equipment	205
Total Weight Used For Tactical Mission	4020

Plane Number 4 · Headquarters Company

Personel Loading	S/N	Hometown	Wt. Fully Equipped
1. Lt. C. E. Spires	O-380643	Hartville, Carolina	248
2. Pfc. George Voleta	36048603	Chicago, Illinois	255
3. Pvt. George J. Sheridan	33110740	Sharon, Pennsylvania	265
4. Pvt. Merse J. Process	33038269	Centerville, Pennsylvania	284
5. Cpl. Joseph W. Lee	20350108	Annapolis, Maryland	277
6. Cpl. Merle L. Shearer	35212348	Wellsburg, West Virginia	272
7. Cpl. Leland R. Hottun	34146066	Memphis, Tennessee	288
8. Cpl. Elehm Puckett	35108893	Irvine, Kentucky	297
9. Pvt. William Cooper	33037842	Cross Creek, Pennsylvania	254
10. Pvt. Charles J. Lovday	35129930	Middlesboro, Kentucky	270
11. Pvt. William J. Holtz	35212885	Ironton, Ohio	236
12. Pvt. Robert L. Thomas	35212714	Pocha, West Virginia	255
13. Sgt. Clarence H. Thomas	34087920	Atlanta, Georgia	244

Total Weight	3455
Equipment Bundle No. 1	279
Equipment Bundle No. 2	289
Total Weight Used	
For Tactical Mission	4023

Plane Number 5 · Headquarters Company

Personel Loading	S/N	Hometown	Wt. Fully Equipped
1. Lt. John W. Teasley	O-422358	Columbus, Georgia	242
2. T-4 George Houston	35103811	Detroit, Michigan	286
3. Pvt. Adolph Fuessel	38034226	Buckholtz, Texas	304
4. Pvt. Stanley B. Gillman	35168247	Brookville, Indiana	261
5. Cpl. Wiley J. Flohr	35166067	Crestline, Ohio	256
6. Cpl. Charles O. Holmes	35168653	Bicknell, Indiana	288
7. Pvt. Vernon O. Walker	34056609	Lmmokalee, Florida	272
8. Pvt. Roland Weeks	34056873	Collier City, Florida	257
9. Pvt. Jack Alongi	36127657	Detroit, Michigan	218
10. Pvt. John T. Pierce	35168604	Walcottville, Indiana	240
11. Pvt. Charles J. Otzel	11019840	Bridgeport, Connecticut	228
12. Pvt. Haskel Hill	34146608	Knoxville, Tennessee	249
13. Pvt. George B. Chaffin	35035981	Springfield, Ohio	256
14. Sgt. Roderick Childs	32028873	Angelica, New York	255

Total Weight	3612
Equipment Bundle Weight	294
Special Equipment	114
Total Weight Used	
For Tactical Mission	4020

Plane Number 6 · Headquarters Company

Personel Loading	S/N	Hometown	Wt. Fully Equipped
1. Sgt. Edward Danish		Chicago, Illinois	294
2. Pvt. Robert Kealen	6918072	Quiney, Illinois	311
3. Pfc. Robert M. Barnthouse	35168853	Decatur, Indianna	272
4. Cpl. Martin L. Ullicny	36127619	Rochester, Pennsylvania	288
5. Pvt. Martin W. Crites	37082538	Kennett, Missouri	251
6. Pvt. Charles Cipy	33108388	Dundalk, Maryland	244
7. Pvt. John F. Robinson	35108558	Louisville, Kentucky	223
8. Pvt. Robert B. Waller	34087987	College Park, Georgia	240
9. Pvt. Russell P. Cook	35175159	Birdseye, Indiana	238
10. Pvt. Paul E. Legg	3516894	Vincennes, Indiana	260
11. Pfc. Harry Phillips	36022005	Moline, Illinois	232
12. Pvt. William Vandenberg	36159887	Grand Rapids, Michigan	261
13. Pvt. Clifford B. Faulkner	35212343	Power, West Virginia	286
14. Cpl. Paul Chorniak	35035688	Buchtel, Ohio	268

Total Weight	3668
Equipment Bundle Weight	280
Special Equipment	72
Total Weight Used For Tactical Mission	4020

Plane Number 7 · Headquarters Company

Personel Loading	S/N	Hometown	Wt. Fully Equipped
1. Lt. Seldon D. Harvey	O-337182	Portage, Wisconsin	263
2. Cpl. Henry R. Pardieck	35129995	Ann, Ohio	250
3. Cpl. Eugene Brewer	34145992	Collierville, Tennessee	262
4. Pfc. Jessee J. Luczyk	35028773	Cleveland, Ohio	279
5. Pfc. Walter Endlich	35028838	Stone Creek, Ohio	284
6. Pfc. George W. Michael	35028954	Mt. Overlook, Ohio	272
7. Pfc. Leonard Swatsenbarg	37139986	Senaca, Maryland	275
8. Pvt. Donald B. Ellis	35168555	Spencer, Indiana	268
9. Pvt. Gerald T. Hogan	36163675	Muir, Michigan	281
10. Pvt. Joseph Bauer	35166160	Evansville, Indiana	267
11. Cpl. Don W. Herrin	34024320	South Bay, Florida	259
12. Pfc. Francis L. Keane	32180425	Brooklyn, New york	249
13. Pfc. Johnny N. Boyce	35212472	Hammond, West Virginia	292
14. Sgt. Wesley Lee	37139895	Winston, Minnesota	247

Total Weight	3748
Equipment Bundle Weight	250
Special Equipment	22
Total Weight Used For Tactical Mission	4020

Plane Number 8 · Headquarters Company

Personel Loading	S/N	Hometown	Wt. Fully Equipped
1. Lt. Hugh G. Hogan	O-1283258	Owego, New York	253
2. Cpl. Edwin G. Wegner	36226687	Miami, Florida	297
3. Pvt. William Southerland	6392752	Gaffney, South Carolina	255
4. Pvt. James H. Ballentine	36127700	Hermitage, Tennessee	266
5. Pvt. Walter T. Borowiak	33111618	Hazelton, Pennsylvania	271
6. Pvt. Joseph W. Cernak	33118496	Johnstown, Pennsylvania	276
7. Pvt. Clare F. Granbit	37111394	Des Moines, Iowa	266
8. Cpl. John T. Martin	34087918	La Grange, Georgia	278
9. Sgt. Elwood Barnhardt	33100791	Philadelphia, Pennsylvania	288
10. Pfc. Fred R. Gerber	38068874	ElPaso, Texas	255
11. Pvt. Ross E. Bittinger	33067321	Essex, Maryland	282
12. Pfc. Guy W. Jeanes	38058524	San Augustine, Texas	274
13. Sgt. John F. Costello	33098475	Washington, D.C.	251
14. S/Sgt. William Campbell	34091991	Sheldon, South Carolina	225

Total Weight	3737
Equipment Bundle Weight	250
Special Equipment	33
Total Weight Used For Tactical Mission	4020

Plane Number 9 · Headquarters Company

Personel Loading	S/N	Hometown	Wt. Fully Equipped
1. Maj. Doyle R. Yardley	O-356190	Raymondsville, Texas	235
2. Lt. Stuart G. Cutler	O-394597	New York, New York	255
3. T-5 Jack A. Wagers	19099001	Brush, Colorado	270
4. Pvt. Arthur W. Von Essen	32120668	Woodhaven, New York	255
5. Pvt. Alphonse A. Zoucha	3816710	Cedar Rapids, Nebraska	287
6. Pvt. Walter A. Cherry	35166807	Eldorado, Arkansas	271
7. Pvt. Lincoln S. Sennett	31044632	Auburn, Me.	247
8. Pvt. Thomas S. Wimberly	34056778	Cochran, Georgia	284
9. Pvt. Robert H. Green	35108666	Cartland, Indiana	253
10. Pvt. Harold Seay	38010161	Roswell, New Mexico	282
11. Pvt. David R. Vail	34145373	Chattanooga, Tennessee	264
12. Pvt. Francis Tocci	6561311	Los Angeles, California	263
13. T-4 Leon C. Maenbout	35169598	Mishawaka, Indiana	235
14. Lt. Timothy			

Total Weight	3667
Equipment Bundle Weight	296
Special Equipment	57
Total Weight Used For Tactical Mission	4020

Plane Number 10 · Headquarters Company

Personel Loading	S/N	Hometown	Wt. Fully Equipped
1. Lt. Hugh C. DeLury	O-1283038	Corry, Pennslyvania	254
2. Pvt. Herbert M. Coberly	33134321	Elkins, West Virginia	264
3. Pvt. Vernon L. Bass	20434753	Dupont, Georgia	254
4. Pvt. Robert T. Byrom	14079420	Huntsville, Alabama	255
5. Pvt. Daniel Brenner	33025780	Philadelphia, Pennsylvania	246
6. Pvt. Donald H. Kammer	34050279	Miami, Florida	241
7. Pvt. William T. Marshall	37053390	Drakesboro, Kentucky	229
8. Pvt. Joseph Barressi	11046075	Sanqus, Massachussits	249
9. Pvt. Leigh F. Fox	37053531	St. Louis, Missouri	231
10. Pvt. John L. Albert	34050284	Miami, Florida	254
11. Pvt. James E. McGrath	36010038	Prairie duChien, Wisconsin	229
12. Pvt. Clifford C. King	6287176	Waco, Texas	231
13. Sgt. James W. Clance	20434271	Port Orange, Florada	236

		Total Weight	3173
		Equipment Bundle Weight	273
		Special Equipment	273
		Total Weight Used	
		For Tactical Mission	4020

Supply Plane Number 1

Personel Loading	S/N	Hometown	Wt. Fully Equipped
1. Capt. Henry C. Tipton	O-376788	Horn Lake, Mississippi	270
2. S/Sgt. Maynard L. Carp	33661114	Baltimore, Maryland	290
3. T-5 John W. Ramsden	34105753	Dora, Alabama	270
4. S/Sgt. Allen W. Stafford	36159288	Hillsdale, Michigan	254
5. S/Sgt. Anthony J. Gorshe	36050397	Perkin, Illinois	270
6. S/Sgt. Silas A. Worley	6576218	Hillsboro, Texas	260
7. T-5 William D. Ates	34106238	Holt, Florida	250
8. T-5 Mifflin G. Glenn	6998604	Catonsville, Maryland	265

		Total Weight	2109
		Special Equipment	1911
		Total Weight Used	
		For Tactical Mission	4020

Supply Plane Number 2

Personel Loading	S/N	Hometown	Wt. Fully Equipped
1. S/Sgt. James C. Whittington	7096236	Oakdale, Louisiana	270
2. T-5 Chester A Thomas	37038517	Valentine, Nebraska	270
3. T-5 Robert B. Cakes	33067118	Capital Heights, Maryland	270
4. T-5 Joseph R. Rambin	34079149	Pelican, Louisiana	250
5. T-5 Harvey G. Peace	34049063	Laurel, Mississippi	240
6. T-5 Robert L. Jones	34106840	Flomanton, Alabama	240
7. T-5 Guadalupe Vasquez	6951835	Brownsville, Texas	250
8. Pvt. Lorenz C. Malberg	17018102	Cokato, Minnesota	270
		Total Weight	2060
		Special Equipment	1960
		Total Weight Used For Tactical Mission	4020

Plane Number 1 · Company "D"

Personel Loading	S/N	Hometown	Wt. Fully Equipped
1. Capt. William J. Morrow	0-349971	Grand Folks, North Dakota	285
2. Pfc. George Matson	34106710	Sylacauga, Alabama	246
3. T-4 Thomas Crane	33082489	Corry, Pennsylvania	253
4. Sgt. Dwight Burns	37110017	Marshalltown, Iowa	254
5. Sgt. Alton Crocker	33082490	Union City, Pennsylvania	265
6. Cpl. Samuel M. Richards	33110658	Avalon, Pennsylvania	246
7. Pfc. Charles Boisvert	37139806	Osawatomie, Kansas	284
8. Pfc. Thadeous Czolgosz	36166550	Saginaw, Michigan	278
9. Pfc. Marvin E. White	35271526	Lima, Ohio	274
10. Pfc. Murphy Trahen	35164996	New Orleans, Louisiana	275
11. Sgt. William Bryson	33094557	Asheville, North Carolina	240
12. Pfc. Marion W. Shade	35127864	Miamisburg, Ohio	289
13. T-5 Elmer R. Maurer	33072099	Philadelphia, Pennsylvania	255
		Total Weight	3457
		Equipment Bundle Weight	250
		Total Weight Used For Tactical Mission	3707

Plane Number 2 · Company "D"

Personel Loading	S/N	Hometown	Wt. Fully Equipped
1. Lt. Charles C. W. Howland	0-399875	Royersford, Pennsylvania	278
2. Pvt. Franklin Briedegan	33075868		
3. Pvt. Thaddeus J. Dabrowski	31025288	Hopedale, Massachusetts	242
4. Pvt. Robert W. McHale	6660751	Clarksburg, West Virginia	257
5. Pfc. Harry E. Tracey	33084490	Pittsburgh, Pennsylvania	253
6. Pvt. John E. Pumphey	34054826	Apopka, Florida	247
7. Pvt. Paul B. Huff	34142155	Cleveland, Tennessee	247
8. Pvt. James W. Nunn	20418468	Jacksonville, Florida	254
9. Russell T. Neview	6910997	Saulte Ste. Marie, Michigan	268
10. Cpl. Richard LaForge	36125239	Au Sable, Michigan	249
11. Richard D. Fisco	6973808	Staten Island, New York	254
12. Sgt. Varna C. Shresberry	35209806	Rhodell, West Virginia	254
13. T-5 Tracey L. McCue	6928880	East Gaston, Alabama	235
14. T-5 Edgar F. Millisite	35026975	Canton, Ohio	240
15. Lt. John V. Jennings	0-1283113	Orange, New Jersey	260

Total Weight	3750
Equipment Bundle Weight	250
Special Equipment	20
Total Weight Used For Tactical Mission	4020

Plane Number 3 · Company "D"

Personel Loading	S/N	Hometown	Wt. Fully Equipped
1. Lt. Robert W. Parker	0-425986	Crowley, Louisiana	225
2. Pfc. Kenneth DeWald	33110909	Williamsport, Pennsylvania	250
3. Pfc. Joseph J. Anslow	20203919	Troy, New York	261
4. S/Sgt. Lehman Lecompt	6928563	Elba, Alabama	240
5. Pfc. Ord E. Elmore	36262071	Walford, West Virginia	287
6. Pvt.Amos W. Wilder	14018975	Newman, Georgia	238
7. Pfc. Carey L. Tidwell	34084255	Atlanta, Georgia	239
8. Pfc. Edwin M. Stapleton	35209762	McComas, West Virginia	228
9. Pvt. Ray Carr	190655063	Hawarden, Iowa	265
10. Pvt. William B. Azline	36164138	Detroit, Michigan	230
11. Pvt. Houston C. Akins	14071587	Chattanooga, Tennessee	244
12. Pfc. Roy R. Barlow	34200089	Crestview, Florida	270
13. Sgt. Carl E. Bigham	36124594	Trenton, Michigan	242
14. Pvt. Carl R. Clegg	33033307	Pittsburg, Pennsylvania	261

Total Weight	3460
Equipment Bundle Weight	250
Special Equipment	290
Total Weight Used For Tactical Mission	4020

Plane Number 4 · Company "D"

Personel Loading	S/N	Hometown	Wt. Fully Equipped
1. 1/Sgt. Vernon T. Cartnay	6931114	Marion, South Dakota	254
2. Sgt. Michael Baranek	35026946	Akron, Ohio	249
3. Pfc. Everett J. Hall	31051063	Riverside, Rdode Island	243
4. Cpl. Leo E. Stambaugh	37087017	Big Horn, Wyoming	279
5. Sgt.Robert P. Akers	33048822	Roanoke, Virginia	276
6. Pvt. Milford L. Dugan	33082388	Muncy, Pennsylvania	265
7. Pvt. Edward H. Crowther	20109261	Providence, Rhode Island	270
8. Pfc. Lenwood R. Choquette	31039928	Northampton, Massachusetts	268
9. Pfc. Vincent J. Kleysteuber	36302910	Patoka, Kansas	262
10. Pfc. Percy R. Collins	34079275	Marthaville, Louisiana	283
11. Pvt. Daniel B. Reardon	20111604	Clinton, Massachusetts	248
12. Pvt. Augustine M. Digiovanni	33098797	Washington, D.C.	237
13. Pvt. Felix B. Marsh	34131349	Fentress, Mississippi	243
14. Pfc. Stanley T. Orzell	33022460	Scranton, Pennsylvania	217

Total Weight	3596
Equipment Bundle Weight	250
Special Equipment	274
Total Weight Used For Tactical Mission	4020

Plane Number 5 · Company "D"

Personel Loading	S/N	Hometown	Wt. Fully Equipped
1. Lt. Casper E. Curtis	O-372914	Norway, Maine	257
2. Pfc. Andrew J. Floyd	14022085	Stapleton, Alabama	292
3. Pfc. Lorenzo Boyd	34106184	Frisco City, Alabama	258
4. T-5 Frank Tilton	34082879	Savannah, Georgia	242
5. S/Sgt. Brad Chalkor (288 Radio)	6964534	Gibson, Georgia	275
6. Sgt. Soloman Weber (288 Radio)	32119797	Masbeth, Long Island, N.Y.	285
7. Pvt. Jack L. White	15010028	McConnellsville, Ohio	254
8. Sgt. Arthur R. Thompson	33063193	Kingston, Maryland	259
9. Pvt. John A. Bickle	37130975	St. Louis, Minnesota	263
10. Pvt. Robert L. Doyle	6946153	York, Pennsylvania	247
11. Pfc. Lester F. Barrett	39304963	Hubbard, Oregon	257
12. Pfc. Clyde S. Branthover	39304965	Astoria, Oregon	248
13. Pvt. Barney O. Debray	34087675	Leary, Georgia	261
14. Pfc. Edward K. McGaffick	6902251	Buffalo, New York	252

Total Weight	3650
Equipment Bundle Weight	250
Number 2 Bundle (288 Radio)	110
Special Equipment	10
Total Weight Used For Tactical Mission	4020

160.

Plane Number 6 - Company "D"'

Personel Loading	S/N	Hometown	Wt. Fully Equipped
1. Capt. Carlos C. Alden	O-381690	Buffalo, New York	251
2. Cpl. Odus M. Wardlow	34079020	Montgomery, Louisiana	240
3. Pvt. Curtis M. Whitehead	34079062	Lake Charles, Louisiana	270
4. 1/Sgt. Frank Jackson	7002491	Wilner, Alabama	245
5. Pfc. George F. Schaffer	37098022	Heron Lake, Minnesota	275
6. Pvt. Charles C. Yanush	33084786	Scranton, Pennsylvania	270
7. S/Sgt. William L. Hooker	14044608	Oak Park Station, Florida	254
8. Sgt. Lincoln Miller	34078849	LaFayette, Louisiana	266
9. Pvt. Roman L. Njewienglowski	36162477	Detroit, Michigan	239
10. Pvt. George J. Brodrick	32096557	Brooklyn, New York	264
11. Pfc. Wallace H. Eaker	6909874	Cleveland, Ohio	263
12. Pvt. Horace StringFellow	34055057	Miami, Florida	251
13. T-5 William R. Jameson	14043285	Greenville, South Carolina	257
14. S/Sgt. Douglas T. Robinson	33084023	Upper Darby, Pennsylvania	218

Total Weight	3521
Equipment Bundle Weight	250
Special Equipment	249
Total Weight Used For Tactical Mission	4020

Plane Number 8 - Company "D"

Personel Loading	S/N	Hometown	Wt. Fully Equipped
1. Lt. William F. Threkheld	O-374478		272
2. Cpl. Elmer T. Cardwell	33095679	Alexandria, Virginia	245
3. Pfc. Raymond L. Brockman	35281711	Ft. Jennings, Ohio	285
4. Pfc. Stanley Beatham	31044588	Lincoln, Maine	235
5. Pvt. Woodrow Browder	6382355	Centurs, Florida	293
6. Pfc. Russell G. Harvey	7083955	Early Branch, South Carolina	236
7. Pvt. Pete Way	34092332	Pinewood, South Carolina	247
8. Pfc. John D. Egri	35040030	Lima, Ohio	266
9. Pfc. Bernard B. Schwarm	36045075	Chicago, Illinois	241
10. Pfc. Richard H. Coleman	37130567	Clarence, Missouri	249
11. Pfc. Walter Barrow	33088485	Elwood City, Pennsylvania	260
12. Sgt. Ernest R. Komula	37098117	Sebeka, Minn.	291
13. Pvt. Alcus Stokes	7080390	Laurel Hill, Florida	267
14. Sgt. Kelly C. Barth	14051683	Claxton, Georgia	256

Total Weight	3641
Equipment Bundle Weight	250
Special Equipment	129
Total Weight For Tactical Mission	4020

Plane Number 9 - Company "D"

Personel Loading	S/N	Hometown	Wt. Fully Equipped
1. Lt. Wilber B. McClintock	O-404855	Memphis, Tennessee	217
2. Pfc. John F. Eichhorn	35168863	Craigville, Indiana	239
3. Sgt. William H. King	6883529	Plainfield, New Jersey	225
4. Pvt. Charles W. Richards	32156809	Bridgeton, New Jersey	250
5. S/Sgt. Walter Rice	35210760	Catlettsburg, Kentucky	286
6. Pfc. John E. Campbell	34093870	Columbia, South Carolina	248
7. Pfc. Alphard L. Barnett	34107556	Red Bay, Mississippi	245
8. Pfc. Albert E. Brown	36163545	Croswell, Michigan	238
9. Pfc. John F. Alexander	37102834	Corning, Arkansas	267
10. Sgt. Ralph Thornton	34105456	Cropwell, Alabama	260
11. Pvt. Johnnie Graham	34093967	Little Rock, South Carolina	231
12. Pvt. Louis C. Burdsel	14053575	Greenville, South Carolina	234
13. Pfc. James M. Martin	32036577	Niagra Falls, New York	259
14. S/Sgt. Jack V. Greene	7001000	Chauncey, Georgia	261

Total Weight	3480
Equipment Bundle Weight	250
Special Equipment	290
Total Weight Used	
For Tactical Mission	4020

Plane Number 1 - Company "E"

Personel Loading	S/N	Hometown	Wt. Fully Equipped
1. Capt. John T. Berry	O-396199	Arkadelphia, Arkansas	296
2. T-4 Paul V. Wilson	52209705	Poca, West Virginia	241
3. Sgt. William E. Powell	35106249	West Baden, Indiana	270
4. Sgt. Edward T. Balcom	34054705	Tampa, Florida	266
5. Sgt. Ralph Maerz	6897807	Philadelphia, Pennsylvania	276
6. T-5 Charles R. Allen	31042205	Westport, Connecticut	300
7. Pfc. George Wetrisko	35281362	Elyria, Ohio	279
8. Pvt. Clarence G. Hawkins	34107483	Pisqan, Alabama	275
9. Pvt. Ira L. Brookins		Columbus, Georgia	255
10. Pvt. Arlie K. Graley	35210562	McCorkle, West Virginia	283
11. Cpl. Wilbert E. Sprenkle	33011736	Farm Grove, Pennsylvania	283
12. Lt. Albert V. Crosby	O-412160	Lochoven, Norfolk, Virginia	261
13. Pvt. John Westerlund		Bradford, Pennsylvania	257
14. Pvt. James L. Rodgers		Madison, Indiana	245

Total Weight	3777
Equipment Bundle Weight	250
Special Equipment	0
Total Weight Used	
For Tactical Mission	4027

162.

Plane Number 2 · Company "E"

Personel Loading	S/N	Hometown	Wt. Fully Equipped
1. Lt. Dave C. Kunkle	O-422431	New York, N.Y.	251
2. T-5 James R. Boyle	6932565	St. Joseph, MO.	244
3. Sgt. Fred E. Harding	33099806	New Castle, Pa.	278
4. Cpl. Robert E. League	33060721	Baltimore, Md.	246
5. Cpl. Loran E. Chambers	36051037	Mt. Sterling, Illinois	279
6. Cpl. Eugene R. Hall	35212666	Bastion, Virginia	239
7. Pvt. Louis Homoki	35281377	Elyria, Ohio	262
8. Pfc. Charles L. Murdoch	34085021	Atlanta, Ga.	243
9. Pfc. Carl D. Miley	14059624	Moorville, Mississippi	247
10. Pvt. John Mackall	35281555	Westville, Ohio	272
11. Pvt. Laverne G. Shulion	36303140	Savannah, Illinois	273
12. Pvt. Andrew Panusko	36302969	Chicago, Illinois	254
13. Pvt. Arden O. Peterson	36303162	Rockford, Illinois	264
14. Pvt. Joseph M.Torpey	36034395	Chicago, Illinois	266

Total Weight	3644
Equipment Bundle Weight	250
Special Equipment	126
Total Weight Used For Tactical Mission	4020

Plane Number 3 · Company "E"

Personel Loading	S/N	Hometown	Wt. Fully Equipped
1. Lt. Charles W. Kurtz	O-430341	Tampa, Florida	244
2. Pfc. Herbert Ferguson	35127032	Elmanton, Kentucky	243
3. Pfc. William C. Price	13007471	Scranton, Pennsylvania	264
4. Pfc. Kalmer G. Thompson	37098075	Ulen, Minnesota	282
5. Pfc. Winfield Schadman	33077188	Emporium, Pennsylvania	246
6. Sgt. Robert B. David	34054782	Atlantic Beach, Florida	253
7. Pvt.William Simons	34054797	Sarasota, Florida	247
8. Pfc. Alvin L. Trumbull	31049833	Windsor, Connecticut	278
9. Cpl. Needham S. Smith	34084914	Eastman, Georgia	244
10. Pfc. Walter E. Graska	37097567	St. Cloud, Minnesota	256
11. Pvt. James C.Meachum	34114042	Burlington, North Carolina	263
12. Pvt. Albert Dager	33118235	Ambler, Pennsylvania	243
13. Sgt. Charlie B. Fuller	6969861	Warm Springs, Florida	287
14. Lt. Joseph J. Winsko	O-386568	Wilkes Barre, Pennsylvania	303

Total Weight	3642
Equipment Bundle Weight	250
Special Equipment	116
Total Weight Used For Tactical Mission	4020

Plane Number 4 · Company "E"

Personel Loading	S/N	Hometown	Wt. Fully Equipped
1. 1st Sgt. John j. Klish	6890139	New Castle, Pennsylvania	267
2. Sgt. Charles W. Hood	34084855	Atlanta, Georgia	280
3. T-5 Howard H. Herr, Jr.	33076970	Lancaster, Pennsylvania	280
4. T-5 James H. Nixon	33094099	Washington, D.C.	254
5. Sgt. Ralph R. Bourn	36043728	Jacksonville, Illinois	296
6. Pfc. Alexander W. Osmond	13004495	Taylor, Pennsylvania	297
7.			
8. Pfc. John H. Cross	34055040	Miami Beach, Florida	270
9. Pfc. William E. Paley	35281449	Youngstown, Ohio	258
10. Pfc. Richard J. Reusching	35027273	Jefferson, Ohio	275
11. Cpl. William E. Barker	34082808	Chickamauga, Georgia	273
12. Pfc. James W. Bates	34054726	Tampa, Florida	219
13. Pvt. Edward C. Holley	35214733	Hamlin, West Virginia	269
14. T-5 Howard E. Laudwig	36303072	St. Louis, Minnesota	256

Total Weight	3752
Equipment Bundle Weight	250
Special Equipment	18
Total Weight Used For Tactical Mission	4020

Plane Number 5 · Company "E"

Personel Loading	S/N	Hometown	Wt. Fully Equipped
1. Lt. Lloyd G. Wilson	O-412416	Micawber, Oklahoma	251
2. Pvt. Franklin J. Hall	31039846	Springfield, Massachusetts	252
3. Pvt. Henry Hamilton	6666603	Ary, Kentucky	272
4. Cpl. Harold D. Ramey	6292081	Los Angeles, California	259
5. Pfc. Lewis L. Jones	17010079	Nettleton, Arkansas	269
6. Pfc. Edward Burns	35168434	Indianapolis, Indiana	266
7. Cpl. George G. Fontanesi	33079760	Library, Pennsylvania	274
8. Pfc. Robert L. Johnson	15098837	Akron, Ohio	232
9. Pfc. Henry G. Cuethle	34054924	West Palm Beach, Florida	238
10. Pvt. James R. Prince, Jr.	34146207	Mt. Pleasant, Tennessee	279
11. Pvt. Earl M. Williamson	3529895	Sistervile, West Virginia	289
12. Pvt. George W. Caldwell	14019108	Manchester, Georgia	269
13. Pvt. Leonard S. Caruso	32134552	New York, New York	245
14. Pvt. Louis J. Catizone	32003189	New York, New York	250

Total Weight	3629
Equipment Bundle Weight	250
Special Equipment	111
Total Weight Used For Tactical Mission	4020

164.

Plane Number 6 · Company "E"

Personel Loading	S/N	Hometown	Wt. Fully Equipped
1. S/Sgt. Paul E. McRill	36043789	Centralia, Illinois	276
2. Sgt. Wilbur D. Martin	32022345	Brooklyn, New York	276
3. Sgt. Charles M. Talbott	34054990	New Smyrna, Florida	256
4. Pvt. Jesse W. Bacon	34084577	Savannah, Georgia	274
5. Pvt. Richard G. Rhoads	34055080	Miami, Florida	263
6. Cpl. Robert V. Patsch	35281825	Sandusky, Ohio	247
7. Pvt. Woodruff F. Wilkerson	35127709	Cincinnati, Ohio	258
8. Pfc. John L. Betts	34054851	Frostproof, Florida	278
9. Pfc. Stanley D. Sjostrom	34055054	Miami, Florida	249
10. Pfc. Hilton E. Graham	34084826	Eastman, Georgia	242
11. Pfc. William B. Poole	34084610	Unadilla, Georgia	264
12. Cpl. Henry C. Faircloth	34084823	Summertown, Georgia	257
13. Pvt. Romas E. Holder	33119420	Dumbarton, Virginia	245
14. S/Sgt. Robert H. Paudert	6972398	Memphis, Tennessee	249

Total Weight	3637
Equipment Bundle Weight	250
Special Equipment	133
Total Weight Used	
For Tactical Mission	133

Plane Number 7 · Company "E"

Personel Loading	S/N	Hometown	Wt. Fully Equipped
1. Lt. Carl E. Dittman		Philadelphia, Pennsylvania	272
2. T-4 Claud H. Purvis	33095532	Washington, D.C.	264
3. Cpl. Elzie B. McCullough	34054816	Bonifay, Florida	238
4. Cpl. Chester Majchrzak	35166596	Gary, Indiana	232
5. Pfc. Carl R. Weaver	33094441	Washington, D.C.	239
6. Pvt. John V. Forni	31839874	Great Barrington, Massachusetts	240
7. Pvt. Harold L. Herbert	33098931	Washington, D.C.	241
8. Pfc. Marion W. Thomas	34054810	Milton, Florida	267
9. Pfc. Hugh D. Camp	34084489	Atlanta, Georgia	254
10. Pfc. Dixie C. Johnson	34054963	Jacksonville, Florida	235
11. Pvt. Lloyd G. Van Guilder	37097654	Fairbault, Minnesota	259
12. Pfc. Alfred R. Groom	20380015	Washington, D.C.	228
13. Pvt. Peter Carsetti	34079162	Seacaucus, New Jersey	281
14. S/Sgt. Uyless V. Haymes	34107117	Cullman, Alabama	

	3546
Total Weight	250
Equipment Bundle Weight	241
Special Equipment	
Total Weight Used	4020
For Tactical Mission	

Plane Number 8 · Company "E"

Personel Loading	S/N	Hometown	Wt. Fully Equipped
1. Lt. Archie G. Birkner	O-416862	San Antonio, Texas	239
2. T-5 Howard N. Macleon	36124569	Port Huron, Michigan	225
3. Sgt. Artrur L. Kellar	6918151	E. Alton, Illinois	270
4. Cpl. Rodger B. Zeigler	34054965	St. Petersburg, Florida	266
5. Pvt. Hyman W. Anderson	14059628	Mt. Olive, Mississippi	271
6. Pfc. Wesley E. Gunderson	16023352	Aniwa, Wisconsin	249
7. Pvt. Charles B. Mask	34084242	Covington, Georgia	262
8. Sgt. Jackson T. Sapp	34107120	Hanceville, Alabama	263
9. Pfc. Clifford E. Fain	34107164	Selma, Alabama	274
10. Pfc. James C. Nesmith	34107194	Venemont, Alabama	264
11. Pfc. James E. Thomason	24106915	Florence, Alabama	262
12. Pfc. Avery Sellers	34084749	Graham, Georgia	260
13. Pvt. Otto Ekman	16023551	Winter, Wisconsin	262
14. Sgt. Robert T. Stier	14044586	Miami, Florida	238

Total Weight	3647
Equipment Bundle Weight	250
Special Equipment	117
Total Weight Used For Tactical Mission	4020

Plane Number 9 · Company "E"

Personel Loading	S/N	Hometown	Wt. Fully Equipped
1. 1st. Sgt. James C. Anderson	6971875	Bowden, Georgia	253
2. Sgt. Dillard T. Winkler	6973622	Roswell, Georgia	280
3. Sgt. Andrew P. Omasta	6664028	Campbell, Ohio	257
4. Pvt. John E. Hendricks	33088812	Washington, D.C.	264
5. Pfc. Julius LeBlanc	34079229	Delcamube, Louisiana	254
6. Pfc. Clyde Thornton	34054835	Raiford, Florida	252
7. Pfc. Burl E. Bolesta	34054670	Tampa, Florida	263
8. Cpl. James B. Ray	34085048	Rome, Georgia	248
9. Pfc. William A. Soska	36309245	Chicago, Illinois	256
10. Pfc. John J. Perry	35281608	Ashtabula, Ohio	254
11. Sgt. William J. Herb	35166498	Coal Bluff, Indiana	264
12. Sgt. Clarence G. Callahen	34054873	Shamrock, Florida	260
13. Pvt. Warren F. Martin	13001329	Crellin, Maryland	245
14. Pvt. William J. Kerney	32172239	Brooklyn, New York	265

Total Weight	3801
Equipment Bundle Weight	250
Special Equipment	153
Total Weight Used For Tactical Mission	4020

166.

Plane Number 1 · Company "F"

Personel Loading	S/N	Hometown	Wt. Fully Equipped
1. Capt. Erven E. Boettner	0-379436	Roca, Nebraska	269
2. T-4 William Sherman	6143428	North Grovendane, Conn.	251
3. Pvt. William O. Wright	33047493		274
4. Pfc. Clifford E. Simonds	34078779	Kinder, Louisiana	280
5. S/Sgt. Joseph Viteritto, Jr.	32156950	Newark, New Jersey	274
6. Pvt. Leroy E. Ande	36159311	Detroit, Michigan	269
7. Pvt. Ocko F. Leonard	34114070	Lexington, N.C.	285
8. Sgt. William E. Moses	33081732	Altoona, Pennsylvania	249
9. Pfc. Archie O. Martin	35048877	Roanoke, Virginia	237
10. Pfc. Charlie A. Smith	33075780	Belle Fonte, Pennsylvania	225
11. Cpl. Samuel M. Flagler	34085397	Kingstree, South Carolina	261
12. Pfc. Leroy E. Dokey	36159299		231
13. T-5 Keith Argraves	39202734	Portland, Oregon	276
14. T/4 Joseph H. Moore	34084125	Sylvania, Georgia	239

Total Weight	3620
Equipment Bundle Weight	250
Special Equipment	150
Total Weight Used For Tactical Mission	4020

Plane Number 2 · Company "F"

Personel Loading	S/N	Hometown	Wt. Fully Equipped
1. Lt. Edmund J. Tomasik	0-373015	New Bedford, massachusetts	260
2. Pfc. William F. Withem	35034953	Glouster, Ohio	281
3. Pfc. Roger P. Derringer	35281777	DeFiance, Ohio	239
4. Pvt. Edwin C. Hicks	34084165	Rockmart, Georgia	254
5. T-5 Dorsey W. Moody	34054702	St. Petersburg, Florida	243
6. Pfc. Leroy Mills	35261846	Middletown, Ohio	257
7. Cpl. Ross W. Clem	34059447	Auburndale, Florida	243
8. Pfc. Demont S. Erland	37109951	Vinton, Iowa	277
9. Pfc. Robert G. Suarez	34106597	Lillian, Alabama	248
10. Pvt. Joseph S. Moffo	33070015	Bristow, Pennsylvania	268
11. Pfc. James R. Hammonds	34085047	Rome, Georgia	228
12. Pfc. Floyd W. Calhoun	34107514	Gordon, Alabama	261
13. Sgt. Ortagus	14013763	Miami, Florida	245
14. Sgt. William H. Simmons	34106608	Fairhope, Alabama	277

Total Weight	3581
Equipment Bundle Weight	250
Special Equipment	189
Total Weght Used For Tactical Mission	4020

167.

Plane Number 3 · Company "F"

Personel Loading	S/N	Hometown	Wt. Fully Equipped
1. Lt. Ralph R. Miller	O-1283116	Youngstown, Ohio	257
2. Pvt. Pete Mrvosh	33111127	Beaver Falls, Pennsylvania	260
3. Pvt. Roger W. Durant	35291735	Canton, Ohio	281
4. Sgt. Carl E. Salisbury	35164991	Frankfort, Indiana	264
5. Pvt. Harry F. Bailey	15060021	Louisville, Kentucky	261
6. Pvt. John F. Hendricks	20649027	Lake Butler, Florida	252
7. Pfc. Adolph Gennarelli	36044975	Chicago, Illinois	257
8. Pvt. J. J. O'Brien	31026494		219
9. Pfc. Marshall E. Mitchell	35212629	Norfolk, West Virginia	253
10. Pfc. Royden V. Vandervort	34055018	Tampa, Florida	229
11. Sgt. Roland Weeks	34056873	Collier City, Florida	281
12. Sgt. Walter L. McCook	6926143	Fitzgerald, Georgia	253
13. Cpl. William H. Leatherwood	34054885	Gainesville, Florida	250
14. T-5 Carroll C. Proctor	36043814	Salem, Illinois	260

Total Weight	3577
Equipment Bundle Weight	250
Special Equipment	193
Total Weight Used For Tactical Mission	4020

Plane Number 4 - Company "F" '

Personel Loading	S/N	Hometown	Wt. Fully Equipped
1. S/Sgt. Tom W. Odom	6971808	Smithville, Georgia	247
2. Pvt. Bernard L. Roberts	34044772	Rockland, Maine	269
3. Pvt. John R. Patton	35212275	Ashland, Kentucky	256
4. Pvt. Earnest E. Nelson	34142154	Knoxville, Tennessee	288
5. Pvt. Henry G. Wilburn	16047429	Milwaukee, Wisconsin	274½
6. Pvt. Theodore J. Kotlowski	33082552	Cambridge Springs, Pennsylvania	278½
7. Sgt. Walter R. Patterson	34140111	Spring Cty, Tennessee	263
8. Pvt. Eugene J. Felippelli	32173166	Flushing, New York	235
9. Pvt. Robert D. Daves	34172325	Drexel, North Carolina	236½
10. Pvt. Harold T Caulfield	26045057	Chicago, Illinois	256
11. Pfc. Rosarie E. Cyr	31048024	Waterbury, Connecticut	233
12. Cpl. Leo C. Inglesby	33072277	Philadelphia, Pennsylvania	251
13. Sgt. Eugene R. Grafe	34052586	St. Petersburg, Florida	277
14. Sgt. Lloyd K. Bjelland	16006665	Taylor, Wisconsin	260

Total Weight	3614½
Equipment Bundle Weight	250
Special Equipment	155½
Total Weight Used For Tactical Mission	4020

Plane Number 5 · Company "F"

Personel Loading	S/N	Hometown	Wt. Fully Equipped
1. Lt. Fred E. Perry	O-395326	Dayton, Ohio	242
2. Pvt. Michael Sembrat	32135740	Syracuse, New York	243
3. Pvt. Lester L. Moore	35209893	New Martinsville, West Virginia	269½
4. T-4 Donald L. Sutton	36159286	North Adams, Michigan	242
5. Pfc. Harold H. Murren	37007994	St. Joseph, Missouri	261½
6. Pvt. Bert E. Dockins	34094078	Fair Play, South Carolina	273
7. Sgt. Frank Pflugler	33077758	Northhampton, Pennsylvania	221
8. Pvt. William D. Cross	34104803	Birmingham, Alabama	252
9. Pvt. Charles E. Parten	34107213	Selma, Alabama	250
10. Pvt. James M. Broadway	34142993	Pope, Tennessee	272
11. Pvt. William I. Eckroth	6945098	Harrisburg, Pennsylvania	239
12. Pvt. Carmine J. Manente	31048564	Hartford, Connecticut	229
13. Sgt. Harold O. Graff	34078495	New Orleans, Louisiana	240½
14. George Olesh, Jr.	33111596	Allentown, Pennsylvania	265

Total Weight	3499
Equipment Bundle Weight	250
Special Equipment	271
Total Weight Used For Tactical Mission	4020

Plane Number 6 · Company "F"

Personel Loading	S/N	Hometown	Wt. Fully Equipped
1. S/Sgt. Lowell W. Frank	12002260	Cuba, New York	243
2. Pfc. Steven Nowakowski	35019974	Toledo, Ohio	245
3. Sgt. Donald E. Davis	6965436	Whistler, Alabama	252
4. Pvt. George Russ	35045525	Canton, Ohio	257
5. Pvt. Kenneth M. Nolte	16047653	Onalaska, Wisconsin	245½
6. Sgt. Edward R. Miller	34054903	Lakeland, Florida	280
7. Pfc. Chester J. Witkowski	33077043	Erie, Pennsylvania	258
8. Pfc. Raymond J. Donovan	37110174	Bernard, Iowa	250
9. Pfc. Thomas F. Dunlavey	310333970	Lowell, Massachusetts	246½
10. Pvt. Russell C. Morris	35126953	Marmet, West Virginia	268
11. Sgt. Joseph L. Buchanan	14017112	Rayville, Louisiana	274
12. Pvt. Marcus Kukee	36231034	Milwaukee, Wisconsin	255
13. Pfc. Robert G. Williams	34114860	Durham, North Carolina	248
14. Sgt. Ray Cagle	39376053	Ellensburg, Washington	270

Total Weight	3591
Equipment Bundle Weight	250
Special Equipment	179
Total Weight Used For Tactical Mission	4020

169.

Plane Number 7 · Company "F"

Personel Loading	S/N	Hometown	Wt. Fully Equipped
1. Lt. James H. Hardy	O-390713	Ecru, Mississippi	277
2. S/Sgt. Orval W. Webb	33093727	Washington, D.C.	297
3. Pvt. C. A. Schenk	35281731		270
4. Sgt. Tony J. Manzella	6660751	Bessemer, Alabama	230
5. Pfc. Kenneth Gridley	34054856	Peony, Florida	223
6. Pvt. William H. Davis	20342259	Cumberland, Maryland	233
7. Pfc. John F. Smith	30214281	Acpinwall, Pennsylvania	244
8. Sgt. Leverne S. Fox	34115127	Boone, North Carolina	237
9. Cpl. John W. McGee	35085021	Cabot, Pennsylvania	246
10. Pfc. Lloyd P. Bourn	36043741	Jackonsville, Illinois	265
11. Pfc. Robert H. Soden	39230111	Los Angeles, California	227
12. Pvt. Ivan A. Cooper	37015304	Lyons, Kansas	254
13. Pvt. Charles R. Coffell	34160317	Huntsville, Alabama	230
14. Cpl. James C. Hughes	34085020	Atlanta, Georgia	252½

Total Weight	3475
Equipment Bundle Weight	250
Special Equipment	295
Total Weight Used For Tactical Mission	4020

Plane Number 8 · Company "F"

Personel Loading	S/N	Hometown	Wt. Fully Equipped
1. Lt. William M. Sherman	O-422279	Council Bluffs, Iowa	238½
2. Pfc. W. C. Collins	20417992	Jacksonville, Florida	287½
3. Pfc. Harold I. Shantie	32044872	Norfolk, New York	287
4. T-5 Ora A. Foster	36162028	Pontiac, Michigan	242
5. J. A. Bernado			268
6. Thomas F. Lustrtitz	35281755	Ravenna, Ohio	257
7. Sgt. Woodrow F. Dunlap	34085011	Rome, Georgia	241½
8. Pvt. Daniel H. Drumbeater	37098085	Gheon, Minnesota	250
9. Cpl. Burnett H. Fite	31527868	Mianesburg, Ohio	252
10. Pfc. Edward R. LeCarpentier	39230124	Washington, D.C.	252
11. Pfc. James W. Bussey	34093948	Modoc, South Carolina	226
12. Pfc. Adger S. Shirley	34093887	Hodges, South Carolina	233
13. Pvt. James S. Whitacre	35188060	Ft. Wayne, Indiana	258
14. Pvt. Charles C. Christensen	9631644	Chicago, Illinois	301

Total Weight	3593
Equipment Bundle Weight	250
Special Equipment	177
Total Weight Used For Tactical Mission	4020

Plane Number 9 · Company "F"

Personel Loading	S/N	Hometown	Wt. Fully Equipped
1. T/Sgt. Lester C. McLaney	6966537	Hartford, Alabama	265
2. Sgt. Arthur E. Dickerson	14022595	Carriere, Mississippi	255
3. T-5 William D. Hubbard	31039938	New York, New York	260
4. T-5 Monroe E. Wills	14018863	Hartford, Alabama	260
5. Lt. Robert C. MacLane	O-403125	Chicago, Illinois	277
6. Pfc. Walter E. Mechowski	32135724	Syracuse, New york	273
7. Pfc. Leon P. Sporish	35157349	Newark, New Jersey	273½
8. Pfc. Ralph E. Colwell	33090495	Roanoke, Virginia	248
9. Pvt. Joseph W. Owens	33009860	Laurel, Maryland	273
10. Pvt. Harley Atkinson	6918127	Metropolis, Illinois	292
11. Pfc. Robert W. Miller	33110651	North Pittsburg, Pennsylvania	242
12. Pfc. C. L. Thomas	33109659		238
13. S/Sgt. Jesse A. Silva	31034086	Provincetown, Massachusetts	255
14. 1st Sgt. Mike O'Brien	6930541	Alden, Minnesota	268

Total Weight	3593
Equipment Bundle Weight	250
Special Equipment	177
Total Weight Used For Tactical Mission	4020

171.

INDEX OF REFERENCES

G

H

I

J

K

L

"Little Colonel" - 101, 122
London - 60, 81
"Lord Haw Haw" - 15
Lourmel - 48, 53
Luftwaffe - 90, 134

M

Maison Blanche Airdrome - 84, 87
Malta - 9, 11
Manila - 15
Maps - route of Aircraft from Land's End - 37, 38
       Area of Airborne Operations Near Oran - 59
       Seizure of Oran 8-10 November - 73, 74
       Youks les Bains Drop Area - 91
Marshal, Lt. Col. George - 81
Manchester - 17
Mast, General Emmanuel - 27
Mechanical navigational aids - 19
Medical pouch - 55
Michaels - 42
Milwaukee - 137
Moir, Captain Bill - 56, 60
M-1 carbine - 119
M-1 rifle - 44
Montgomery - 9
Moroccan terrain - 47
Moscow - 9

N

NATO - 20
Navy air personnel - 80
Nazi radar - 40
Night navigation lights - 18
Norfolk House - 15, 17, 19
Normandy Peninsula - 17
Norstadt, Lt. Col. Lauris - 20
North Africa - 20, 25, 27, 47, 53, 60, 95, 108
Northern Ireland - 30
No. 1 Cumberland Place, London - 19

O

Oberdorf, Major John - 39, 48
Obstacle courses - 16
Oran - 17, 19, 28, 40, 42, 81, 91
Oran road - 52, 78
Oued Mellegue - 90
"Overlord" - 11

P

Pacific - 20

Phillips
Publications

The hallmark of Phillips Publications is the ST-23 fighting knife designed and hand forged by William F. Moran, Jr. The ST-23 represents the finest in design, craftsmenship and concern.

Philips Publications is dedicated to the preservation and recording of this country's military history. We maintain a special interest in American military elite units, such as Paratroopers, Rangers, Special Forces, Raiders, O.S.S. etc.

Phillips Publications devotes extensive effort to all details of the manufacturing and design of our products. It is the publisher's desire to produce products that are satisfactory as to their physical qualities and artistic possibilities while keeping in mind our obligation to preserve our nation's history.

WANTED:

WW II through Viet Nam military elite items from O.S.S., 1st S.S.F., Airborne and Ranger Units. Also Recondo, Special Forces, LRRP and SEAL items.
Interested in military fighting knives, photographs, documents, books, equipment, uniforms and weapons.
These items being sought for the collection of the Antietam National museum, Sharpsburg, Maryland.
Research also being made for forthcoming U.S. Military elite unit plate series, and reprint book series.
Information and items needed for forthcoming books on WW II U.S. Airborne uniforms and equipment book, and U.S. Special Forces book.

Jim Phillips - Publisher
P.O. Box 168
Williamstown, N.J. 08094

180.

The author in Italy, 1944, now commanding the elite 509th Parachute Infantry Bn. Some uniform items of note. He designed the paratroopers jumpsuit and the parachute badge worn on his left side jacket. He also designed the new insignia for the 5th Army shoulder sleeve insignia. Little known, Yarborough was the first American to parachute wearing the new steel helmet. Done at Ft. Benning in 1941, over the dire warnings of doctors who predicted that the wind shear would break his neck. Several improvements were made to the M-1 steel pot as a result.

MAISON CARRÉE - Nouvelle Ecole Primaire
Supérieure de Garçons

Masion Carree — The school used by the 509th while quartered in Algeria.

This is the original communications section. Kneeling is Sgt. Pogue who is referred to in this book, is the brand-new 2d Lt., kneeling in the front row. Next to him Sgt. Brad Chaulker. Both wear the Model 1941 jumpsuit. This photo was taken in England, outside Lt. Col. Raff's headquarters.

Marquis Who's Who in America in 1998

YARBOROUGH, WILLIAM PELHAM, writer, lecturer, retired Army officer, consultant: b. Seattle, May 12, 1912; s. Leroy W. and Addessia (Hooker) Y.: m. Norma Mae Tuttle. Dec. 26, 1936: children: Norma Kay (dec.), William Lee, Patricia Mae. BS, U.S. Mil. Acad., 1936; grad., Command and Gen. Staff Coll., 1944, Brit. Staff Coll., 1950. Army War Coll., 1953. Commd. 2nd Lt. U.S. Army, 1936, advanced through grades to Lt. Gen., 1968, ret., 1971; various assignments U.S. Army, U.S., Philippines and ETO, 1936-42; exec. officer Paratroop Task Force, North Africa, 1942; comdr. 2d Bn., 504th Par. Inf. Regt., 82d Airborne Div., Sicily invasion, 1943, 509th Parachute Inf., Italy and France, 1943-44; comdg. officer 473 Inf., Italy, 1945; provist marshal 15th Army Group, ETO, 1945, Vienna Area Command and U.S. Forces, Austria, 1945-47; mem. staff, faculty U.S. Army Info. Sch., 1948-49; operations officer, gen. staff Joint Mil. Assistance Adv. Group, London, Eng., 1951-52; mem. faculty Army War Coll., 1953-56, 57; dep. chief Mil. Assistance and Adv. Group, Cambodia, 1956-57; comdg. officer 66th CIC Group, Stuttgart, Germany, 1958-60, 66th M.I. Group, Stuttgart, 1960; comdg. gene. U.S.A. Spl. Warfare Ctr.: also comdt. U.S. Army Spl. Warfare Sch., Ft. Bragg, 1961-65; sr. mem. UN Command Mil. Armistice Commn., Korea, 1965; asst. dep. chief staff DCSOPS for spl. operations Dept. Army, Washington: chmn. U.S. delegation Inter-Am. Def. Bd., Joint Brazil U.S. Def. Commn., Joint Mexican-U.S. Def. Commn.: Army mem. U.S. sect. permanent Joint Bd. on Def., Can.-U.S. Def. Commn., Washington, 1965; asst. chief of staff intelligence Dept. Army Washington, 1966-68; comdg. gen. I Corps Group, Korea, 1968-69; chief staff, also dep. comdr.-in-chief U.S. Army, Pacific, Hawaii, 1969-71. Contbr. Internat. Mil. and Def. Ency., 1993, MacMillan Ency. of the Am. Mil. 1994; William P. Yarborough collection papers and artifacts donated to Mugar Meml. Librs., Boston U. Decorated Disting. Svc. medal with three oak leaf clusters. Silver Star, Legion of Merit with three oak leaf clusters, Bronze Star, Joint Svc. Commendation medal with oak leaf clusters, Croix de Guerre with Palm (France), Cross for Valor and Diploma (Italy), Order of Merit Second Class (Korea), Order of Ulchi (Korea). Fellow Co. Mil. Historians. Explorers Club; mem. Kiwanis Club. Home: 160 Hillside Rd., Southern Pines, NC 28387-6727.